INCORPORATION AND BUSINESS GUIDE
FOR ONTARIO
How to form your own corporation

M. Stephen Georgas, LL.B.

Self-Counsel Press
(a division of)
International Self-Counsel Press Ltd.
Canada   U.S.A.

Printed in Canada
First edition: August, 1972
Second edition: May, 1974
Third edition: July, 1976
Fourth edition: April, 1979
Fifth edition: February, 1981
Sixth edition: January, 1984
Seventh edition: May, 1985
Eighth edition: September, 1986
Ninth edition: March, 1988
Tenth edition: November, 1989

Canadian Cataloguing in Publication Data

Georgas, M. Stephen, 1949-
    Incorporation & business guide for Ontario

    (Self-counsel legal series)
    First-5th eds. by Jack D. James
    ISBN 0-88908-374-6

    1. Incorporation — Ontario — Popular works.
    2. Private companies — Ontario — Popular works.
    I. Title.   II. Series.
    KE0403.Z82J35 1989   346.713'06622   C89-091568-7

Self-Counsel Press
(a division of)
International Self-Counsel Press Ltd.
Head and Editorial Office
1481 Charlotte Road
North Vancouver, British Columbia V7J 1H1

U.S. Address
1704 N. State Street
Bellingham, Washington 98225

AVAILABLE FROM THE PUBLISHER

In order to incorporate yourself, you will need to file certain forms. You may type these yourself, but it is easier and quicker to use pre-printed forms. The practice has grown in the legal profession of using certain standard printed forms that ease the typing load considerably. The pre-packaged forms are available where you bought this book or you may use the order form on page vi. The cost of each package is $14.95.

The set includes:

2 sets of Articles of Incorporation
2 sets of by-laws
5 share certificates
2 Consent to Use Name of Individual forms
2 Consent to Use Name of Partnership forms
2 Consent to Use Name of Corporation forms
2 Consent to Act as First Director forms

Also available are the following items:

Company seal — $35.00

(The seal should not be ordered until you have received your Certificate of Incorporation.)

Minute book — $17.95

Deposit stamps — "For Deposit Only to the Credit of _____ " — $14.25
(Company name)

Endorsement stamp — "Company Name" — $10.50

Name and address stamp — $16.95

Extra share certificates — 50¢ each

Note: Please allow 3 to 4 weeks for parcel post delivery.

Prices are subject to change without notice.

(Clip and mail)

- -

ORDER FORM

Please send the following items prepaid:

_____ Package form kit $14.95

_____ Seal $35.00

_____ Minute book $17.95

_____ Deposit stamp (with 2 lines) $14.25

_____ Endorsement stamp $10.50

_____ Name and address stamp $16.95

_____ Extra share certificates — 50¢ each   _____

Add $2.50 for postage and handling   _____

$ _____

TOTAL to be forwarded by cheque or money order
or, if you prefer, charge it to your Visa or MasterCard. Please fill in card number and
dates indicated below.

Please send the items checked above to:

Mr./Ms. _____

Address: _____

City: _____ Province: _____ Postal Code:_____

Telephone: _____

Name of corporation: _____

Corporation address (for stamp) if not same as above: _____

Visa/MasterCard Number _____

Validation date_____ Expiry date _____

**Please check your seals and stamps upon receipt. We will not be responsible for errors
reported more than 30 days after mailing.**

For a free catalogue of other Self-Counsel books, write to the address above.

CONTENTS

LIST OF SAMPLES

PREFACE

The purpose of this book is to provide sufficient information of a legal and practical nature to assist you in understanding incorporation procedures and to enable you to incorporate your own corporation.

It also contains information on keeping records up to date following incorporation.

The book applies to a corporation that does not offer its securities to the public — in other words, the "private corporation."

By explaining each step of an actual incorporation, the book will not only enable you to incorporate your own corporation, but also provide information that will be of assistance in maintaining the corporate status. Once incorporated, several matters must be attended to on a continual basis in order to preserve the corporate status.

If questions of a more complicated nature arise such as tax, estate planning, shareholders' agreements, or basic structural corporate changes, you should seek competent legal and accounting advice.

By following the procedures set out in this book, you can save a substantial amount in legal fees for incorporating a corporation.

It is recommended that competent professional help be sought as your business grows and with it your need for legal, accounting, financial and other advice.

In this respect, the publication is not meant to circumvent or to derogate from the value of professional help. It is meant as an aid to people who desire to incorporate and who simply want to become acquainted with the legal and practical implications of incorporation.

From the outset you should ensure that proper accounts and records are set up.

The incorporation procedures set out in the book apply only to "profit-making" businesses, not clubs, social corporations, co-operatives, credit unions, or the like.

The act governing the incorporation of businesses is administered by the Ministry of Consumer and Commercial Relations, Companies Branch, whose members have been most co-operative and helpful in providing valuable assistance.

NOTICE TO READERS

Laws are constantly changing. Every effort is made to keep this publication as current as possible. However, neither the author nor the publisher can accept any responsibility for changes to the law or practice that occur after the printing of this publication. Please be sure you have the most recent edition.

1

INTRODUCTION TO THE INCORPORATED BUSINESS

You are probably already engaged in a small business or are thinking about starting one up, either by yourself or with someone else. One of the first decisions to be made in dealing with the question of starting a business is whether your business "vehicle" should be an individual proprietorship, partnership (two or more persons), or a limited corporation.

a. METHODS OF CARRYING ON BUSINESS

If you are already carrying on business and are not incorporated, you must be operating either as a sole proprietor or as a partner in a business.

At this point it is important to realize that there are only three ways to carry on any business, from the smallest corner grocery store to General Motors of Canada Limited. There are also special entities in existence, such as organizations engaged in charitable or semi-charitable enterprises. These do not concern us here and will not be discussed.

1. The sole proprietorship and partnership

You are free to carry on business under practically any name you or your partners choose, subject to a possible "passing off" action for appropriating someone else's name, or trade mark infringement action.

It is important to realize, however, that the law does not recognize the name of a proprietorship or partnership and, in any legal action, the proprietor and/or partners must be named personally.

For example, Joe Citizen, carrying on business as XYZ GROCERY, if sued, would be named as "JOE CITIZEN carrying on business under the firm name and style of XYZ GROCERY." The legal consequences of carrying on business in this fashion are explained later on.

The assets of a proprietorship or partnershp belong to the individual parties and not to the business. Further, parties carrying on business, either as a proprietorship or partnership, are personally liable for any debts they incur through the business in favor of third party creditors.

In addition, partners are fully liable for debts incurred by each other while acting in the course of business, i.e., they are jointly and severally liable, regardless of the proportionate capital contribution of the individual parties.

It is important to realize that you may be deemed to be in partnership with someone even though you have made no formal declaration of such a partnership. (See instructions for formal declaration in Sample #1.) This is because a partnership is created by the relationship of the parties and not by any formal act or documents signed by the parties.

You can register a proprietorship or partnership with the Minister of Consumer and Commercial Relations by completing a simple computer card available from the department and paying $50.

There is no established test as to what constitutes a partnership, although the following questions are a guide.

(a) Is there a sharing of net profits and losses?
(b) Do any of the parties act as agents for the others?
(c) Is there any property held in joint tenancy?
(d) Is there any implication of partnership on your firm's letterhead or in its correspondence?
(e) Is the nature of the work relationship that of a partnership?

SAMPLE #1
BUSINESS NAMES REGISTRATION FORM

1 2 3 4	1 2 3 4	1 2 3 4	1 2 3 4	1 2 3 4	1 2 3 4	1 2 3 4	1 2 3 4	1 2 3 4
1978/87	1979/88	1980/89	1981/90	1982/91	1983/92	1984/93	1985/94	1986/95

(V) Ontario — Ministry of Consumer and Commercial Relations

BUSINESS OR PARTNERSHIP REGISTRATION

THE PARTNERSHIPS REGISTRATION ACT.
FORM CD-375 07075
(01/80)

1. NAME OF PARNERSHIP OR BUSINESS

J + J INDUSTRIES

2. MAILING ADDRESS (SEE INSTRUCTION 3 & 4)

1720 Eglington Street, E.
Toronto, Ontario ZIP 0G0

POSTAL CODE **Z1P 0G0**

3. BUSINESS ADDRESS (IF DIFFERENT THAN MAILING ADRESS) (SEE INSTRUCTION 3)

POSTAL CODE

MINISTRY USE ONLY
REGISTRATION DATE

EXPIRY DATE

4. DATE OF ESTABLISHING BUSINESS OR PARTNERSHIP MONTH. DAY. YEAR

January 7, 198—

☐ CHECK IF RENEWAL OR CHANGE

5. BUSINESS ACTIVITY CARRIED ON

ANTIQUE BOTTLE SALES

INSTRUCTIONS

1. THE REGISTRATION FEE IS $10 PAYABLE TO THE TREASURER OF ONTARIO. DO NOT SEND CASH THROUGH THE MAIL. CHEQUES MUST BE CERTIFIED.

2. TYPE OR PRINT ONLY AND DO NOT FOLD OR DAMAGE THE FORM.

3. ALL ADDRESSES MUST BE IN FULL, GIVING STREET AND NUMBER OR R.R. NUMBER, MUNICIPALITY OR POST OFFICE, PROVINCE AND POSTAL CODE. P.O. BOX NUMBER IS NOT ACCEPTABLE IN ITEM 3 AND IN ITEM 7 'B'.

4. ALL CORRESPONDENCE FROM THIS OFFICE RELATING TO THIS REGISTRATION INCLUDING THE EXPIRY NOTICE AND THE CERTIFICATE OF REGISTRATION WILL BE MAILED TO THE ADDRESS SHOWN IN ITEM 2 IF THE PERSON FILING REQUIRES IT TO BE MAILED TO HIM AT AN ADDRESS OTHER THAN AS SET OUT IN ITEM 2 A SELF ADDRESSED ENVELOPE OF THE APPROPRIATE SIZE SHOULD BE ENCLOSED.

5. WHERE A MEMBER IS UNDER 18, HIS BIRTHDATE MUST BE SHOWN IN ITEM 7 'A' WITH HIS NAME.

6. CORPORATE PARTNERS MUST INDICATE THEIR CORPORATE CORPORATION NUMBER IN ITEM 7 'A' OTHER NAME AND SET OUT TITLE OF SIGNING OFFICER IN ITEM 7 'D'.

7. PLEASE CHECK THE APPLICABLE BOX. A LIMITED PARTNERSHIP COMPRISES ONE OR MORE GENERAL 'PARTNERS', JOINTLY AND SEVERALLY RESPONSIBLE AS SUCH AND ONE OR MORE LIMITED PARTNERS WHO CONTRIBUTE CAPITAL BUT ARE NOT LIABLE FOR PARTNERSHIP DEBTS BEYOND THEIR CAPITAL CONTRIBUTIONS. SEE THE LIMITED PARTNER-SHIPS ACT. IN ITEM 7 'C' LIMITED PARTNERS MUST SHOW THEIR CONTRIBUTION TO CAPITAL.

THIS REGISTRATION EXPIRES IN FIVE YEARS BUT MAY BE RENEWED. RENEWAL IS YOUR RESPONSIBILITY. THE REGISTRATION EXPIRY DATE WILL BE SHOWN IN YOUR CERTIFICATE OF REGISTRATION. THE REGISTRATION DOES NOT CONFER ON THE PARTNERSHIP OR PROPRIETOR-SHIP ANY RIGHT TO THE NAME OR STYLE THAT IT DOES NOT OTHERWISE HAVE.

COMPLETE QUESTIONS ON THE REVERSE ▶

THE REGISTRATION HAS NOT BEEN ACCEPTED FOR THE FOLLOWING REASONS:

☐ THE FEE OF $10 WAS NOT ENCLOSED.
☐ THE CHEQUE IS POST-DATED, STALE DATED, NOT DATED, NOT SIGNED
☐ THE CHEQUE MUST BE CERTIFIED AND PAYABLE TO THE TREASURER OF ONTARIO
☐ LATE REGISTRATION - OVER 60 DAYS - AFFIDAVIT REQUIRED
☐ THE FORM HAS NOT BEEN FULLY COMPLETED IN ITEM NUMBER
☐ SEE INSTRUCTION NUMBER
☐ THE INFORMATION IS NOT LEGIBLE OR NOT SUITABLE FOR MICROFILMING
☐ THIS FORM HAS BEEN FOLDED OR DAMAGED
☐

SAMPLE #1
(BACK)

6. ALL MEMBERS OF THE PARTNERSHIP/THE PROPRIETOR WHERE NATURAL PERSONS ARE 18 YEARS OF AGE OR OVER, EXCEPT THOSE WHOSE BIRTHDATE APPEARS IN COLUMN 'A' OF ITEM 7.

7. THE NAMES AND PARTICULARS OF ALL PARTNERSHIP MEMBERS/OR THE PROPRIETOR

A. NAME IN FULL (including all given names)	B. RESIDENCE ADDRESS OR ADDRESS FOR SERVICE (see instruction 3)	TYPE OF PARTNERSHIP C. ☒ General ☐ Limited (SEE INSTRUCTION 7)	D. SIGNATURE
John Deer Doe	#101 - 1200 ORIOLE PKWY Toronto, Ontario ZIP 0G0	IF LIMITED PARTNER CONTRIBUTION TO CAPITAL $	John Deer Doe
Jack Buck Doe	28 Canzone Drive Scarborough, Ont. ZIP 0G0	IF LIMITED PARTNER CONTRIBUTION TO CAPITAL $	Jack Buck Doe
		IF LIMITED PARTNER CONTRIBUTION TO CAPITAL $	
		IF LIMITED PARTNER CONTRIBUTION TO CAPITAL $	
		IF LIMITED PARTNER CONTRIBUTION TO CAPITAL $	
		IF LIMITED PARTNER CONTRIBUTION TO CAPITAL $	
		IF LIMITED PARTNER CONTRIBUTION TO CAPITAL $	

2. The corporate entity and advantages to incorporating

Many people prefer to carry on business as a corporation because of the unique characteristics of a corporate entity. A corporation is a distinct legal entity, an artificial person quite different from the people who are its shareholders. When you incorporate, you actually create a new person in the eyes of the law. The assets and debts of a corporation belong to it — not to the individual shareholders. Because of this characteristic, there are four major advantages for people who incorporate their businesses.

(a) There is potentially a greater source of capital available than in a partnership. Since the company is a "person" separate from its shareholders, people may invest money in it without accepting any further responsibility for conducting the company business and without worrying about becoming liable for the debts of the "company."

(b) Since the corporation is a separate "person," it does not expire when the shareholders die. Substantial estate planning benefits result from this aspect of corporations.

(c) The most advantageous and unique characteristic of a corporation is its limited liability, and this is why corporations are referred to as "limited companies." The words "Limited" "Limitée" "Ltd." or "Ltée," Incorporated" "Incorporée" or "Inc.," "Corporation" or "Corp." must appear in the names of all corporations.

This means that you as a shareholder, with certain exceptions, are not liable for any act, default, obligation or liability of the corporation. This is obviously an important advantage to you. There are, however, certain practical considerations, the most important one being that, in many instances, creditors, particularly banks, will not extend credit to a small corporation without your personal guarantee as its shareholder. However, if you do not personally guarantee your corporation's loans then your liability as a shareholder is limited.

The following examples illustrate the foregoing principles:

Example 1

John Doe and Jack Doe carry on business as a partnership known as J & J Industries.

J & J Industries incurs debts of $25 000.

The assets of J & J Industries are $10 000.

A creditor successfully petitions J & J Industries into bankruptcy or simply gets a judgment against J & J Industries.

All the assets of John Doe and Jack Doe, as individuals, including possibly their homes, cars, etc., may be executed against to repay the $15 000 debt incurred by the partnership over and above its assets.

Example 2

John Doe and Jack Doe carry on business as a corporation known as J & J Industries Limited, with John Doe and Jack Doe the only shareholders, each having purchased one share at $1 (although any number of shares can be purchased).

J & J Industries Limited incurs debts of $25 000.

The assets of J & J Industries Limited are considered to have a market value of $10 000.

A creditor successfully petitions J & J Industries Limited into bankruptcy.

The creditors can realize $10 000 on the assets of the corporation but they have no rights against John and Jack as individuals, regardless of the value of personal assets that John and Jack may own outside the corporation. The creditors are creditors of the corporation, not of John and Jack.

In arranging credit with a financial institution, it may be advisable, if not necessary, to arrange for life insurance on the lives of the shareholders. Depending on how the policy is arranged, different income tax consequences may arise, and professional advice should be sought.

(d) The tax advantages of incorporating are so important that a whole chapter has been devoted to the subject (see chapter 2).

To summarize, then, there are three main legal forms an organization can take. These forms, and their individual characteristics, are outlined briefly below for quick reference.

Proprietorship
(a) Unincorporated
(b) Owned by one person
(c) Creditors have a legal claim on both the investment in the business and the personal assets of the owner

Partnership
(a) Unincorporated
(b) Each partner has unlimited liability in a general partnership arrangement
(c) The acts of one partner in the course of the management of the business are binding upon the other partners
(d) The partnership dissolves upon the death or withdrawal of any partner, or upon the acceptance of a new partner
(e) Creditors have a legal claim on both the investment in the business and the personal assets of the owners

Corporation
(a) Incorporated in most provinces by Memorandum of Association or Articles of Incorporation or federally by Articles of Incorporation
(b) Exists as a separate legal entity
(c) **Shareholders are not liable for any act, default, obligation, or liability of the corporation, with certain exceptions.**
(d) May possess tax advantages

3. Disadvantages to incorporating

First, operating through a corporation does entail extra paperwork. You have to file minutes and keep registers. You have to file two tax returns: one for your corporation and one for yourself. There may be additional government paperwork to do from time to time, which could be avoided by operating as a sole proprietor. Also, there is the cost of setting up and maintaining a minute book and records office (see chapter 5).

Second, any active business income in excess of $200 000 per year does not enjoy the small business tax incentive; income at this level attracts normal corporate tax rates.

However, I assume that this situation applies to so few of us that further comment is unnecessary.

Third, there is the cost and bother of doing the incorporating. By the time you are finished, you will have spent **approximately $400 and a few hours of your time. Is it worth it? Only you can judge.**

b. FINANCIAL STATEMENTS AND THEIR IMPORTANCE

Regardless of what the law says and no matter what legal form an organization may take, the preparation of meaningful financial statements is vital to any enterprise. This is because various people will have an interest in the financial affairs of the organization, namely, owners, managers, creditors, Revenue Canada, and prospective buyers. To illustrate, let us assume that you are a bank manager and that J & J Industries Limited, a medium-sized corporation in the business of manufacturing, approaches you for a $10 000 loan. The principals explain that the funds are necessary for plant expansion. As a prospective creditor you would be interested in two things: the ability of J & J Industries Limited to pay the regular instalments of principal and interest on the loan and the amount you — the bank — would recover if the company could not meet its obligation. To satisfy your curiosity in this regard, you would have to examine the financial statements of the corporation. The annual income would be shown on the profit and loss statement. This figure, if compared with the income from prior periods, would indicate to you the rate of economic growth of the enterprise.

In addition you would be able to determine whether or not enough total revenue is generated to repay the proposed loan. The balance sheet of the corporation would indicate any other long-term debt for which the corporation is liable. Furthermore, you would be able to determine which assets (inventories, accounts receivable, etc.) are available as security for the proposed loan.

The corporation's ability to pay its current obligations is another important indicator of the economic health of the enterprise. This ability to pay present debts when due can also be determined from the balance sheet. This indicator is expressed as a ratio (called the "current ratio") and is calculated by dividing the total of the current assets by the total current liabilities. This is illustrated with the very simple example in Sample #2.

Current assets exceed current liabilities in the ratio of 2:1. In other words, the working capital position of the company in this case is healthy.

In summary, you would obtain much of the information so vital to your decision regarding the loan by looking at the financial statements of J & J Industries Limited.

This illustration shows how financial statements can be useful to potential creditors. Furthermore it is important to realize that financial statements are useful to anyone who has an interest (monetary or otherwise) in an enterprise. To analogize: just as certain medical implements are the tools by which a doctor can get some indication of physical health, so financial statements are the tools by which interested parties can measure the economic health of an organization.

Below is a breakdown, in point form, of the three major financial statements: the balance sheet, the profit and loss statement, and the earned surplus statement. They are discussed here to enable you to get some idea of the function and contents of financial statements.

1. Balance sheet

The balance sheet is a position statement, not an historical record, and shows what is owned and owed at a given date.

There are three sections to a balance sheet: assets, liabilities, and owner's equity.

SAMPLE #2
BALANCE SHEET (Partial)

J & J INDUSTRIES LIMITED

March 31, 198-

Current Assets		Current Liabilities	
Cash	$20 000	Trade payables	$100 000
Accounts receivable	290 000	Wages payable	10 000
Inventories	90 000	Current portion of long term debt	90 000
TOTAL	$400 000	TOTAL	$200 000

(a) Assets

Current assets are those assets which will be used up within one year of the current balance sheet date. Normal valuation of such assets is at original cost or market value, whichever is lower.

Fixed assets are those assets that will provide benefits to the organization over a longer period than one year from the current balance sheet date. Valuation is generally at original cost less accumulated depreciation. The amount of depreciation is based on the length of the useful life of the asset and the original cost of the asset.

To illustrate:

Building: original cost $20 000
Useful life: 10 years
Portion of asset cost which expires in each period:

$$\frac{\$20\,000}{10} = \$2\,000$$

This type of depreciation is normally calculated on a reducing balance basis but for illustrative purposes I have used the straight line method. The sum of $2 000 is charged to the profit and loss statement in each period and is accumulated on the balance sheet as a reduction of the original cost of the asset. Thus, five years after the building was purchased, the balance sheet would show:

Building, at cost	$20 000
Less accumulated depreciation (5 x $2 000)	10 000
Book value of building	$10 000

Because the asset may be sold for more than original cost, the book value does not necessarily indicate the amount the equity-holders should receive for their ownership of the building. (Note: the "equity-holders" in a corporation are the shareholders.)

(b) Liabilities and owner's equity

The nature of these items becomes evident in the illustrations of a typical balance sheet shown in Sample #3.

2. Profit and loss statement

This statement indicates the profit or loss by subtracting the total expenses of a period from the total revenue for that period. There are two ways of determining when revenue is earned and when expenses are incurred. They are:

(a) Cash basis — No revenue is recognized until cash is received. No expenses are recognized until cash is paid out.

(b) Accrual basis — Revenue is recognized as soon as it is earned. Expenses are recognized as soon as they are incurred. The date cash is received or paid out is irrelevant.

3. Earned surplus statement

This statement shows what happens to net profit. The last figure on a balance sheet represents earned surplus. This is the part of previous earnings that is retained by the corporation after providing for reserves and paying all operating expenses, accrued interest (on longer loans), income taxes, and dividends. The earned surplus belongs to the shareholders, but it is retained in the operation as a cushion to absorb possible losses, to protect the corporation from any other unforeseen occurrences, and as part of the capital of the operation.

These statements would be prepared by your accountant from the entries made in your books. In most cases the bank would not require them to be audited. If you were going to offer your shares to the public, the Securities Commission would require you to present audited financial statements.

In the minutes of a shareholders' meeting, you will in most cases waive the appointment of an auditor. Keep in mind this has nothing to do with hiring an accountant to supervise the day-to-day financial affairs of your company. However, hiring an accountant does not have to be discussed and recorded in the minutes of shareholders' meetings like waiving or appointing an auditor does.

c. WHERE TO INCORPORATE

Since a corporation is an artificial person it must be created by someone. A corporation may be incorporated or

ASSETS

Current Assets

Cash on hand and in bank	$ 720.12	
Accounts receivable less allowance for doubtful accounts	657.72	
Merchandise inventory valued at the lower of original cost or market	3 212.63	
Prepaid expenses	157.55	
Total current assets		$4 748.02

Fixed Assets — At Cost

Land		$2 320.00	
Building	$5 767.16		
Less: accumulated depreciation	1 727.92	4 039.24	
Store fixtures	3 726.12		
Less: accumulated depreciation	982.36	2 743.76	
Delivery truck	2 760.20		
Less: accumulated depreciation	513.60	2 246.60	$11 349.60
			$16 097.62

LIABILITIES & PARTNERS' EQUITY

Current Liabilities

Trade accounts payable	$2 772.18	
Accrued wages	75.20	
Employees' income tax payable	60.16	
Accrued real estate taxes	220.00	
Total current liabilities		$3 127.54

Earned Surplus of Partners' Equity*

Jones' share	$6 484.84	
Smith's share	$6 484.84	
		$12 969.68
		$16 097.22

---

*If incorporated this would read as follows:

CAPITAL STOCK
Common stock, no par value, maximum selling price $1
Authorized — 10 000 shares

Issued and fully paid for:
Jones — 50 shares at $0.01 = $0.50
Smith — 50 shares at $0.01 = $0.50

Retained earnings $12 969.68

You will note that Jones and Smith still have equity of a total of $12 969.68.

"born" by a federal charter granted under the Canada Business Corporations Act, or by a provincial certificate under the Business Corporations Act, 1982.

The advantage of incorporating federally is that the corporation has the capacity of a natural person and protection of its corporate name on a nationwide basis. A provincially incorporated corporation is a "person" only in its own province, although there are provisions for registration in other provinces.

For most "non-public," i.e., small, private, family-owned and operated corporations, it is much more convenient to incorporate a provincial corporation. This book will deal with Ontario corporations only.

d. PUBLIC versus PRIVATE CORPORATIONS

For purposes of Ontario corporation law, companies can be of three types: listed corporations, non-listed offering corporations, or closely held (private) non-offering corporations.

1. Listed corporations

Under this category are included most of the well-known, large public corporations whose stock is actively traded on one or more recognized stock exchanges. This book does not discuss the incorporation of this type of organization.

2. Non-listed offering corporations

Under this category are included all corporations whose shares are "publicly" held but, for one reason or another, are not listed and traded on a recognized stock exchange. The most common example is the over-the-counter stock.

This book does not cover the incorporation of this type of organization either because, technically, such corporations are "public" as far as the Securities Commission is concerned and, as such, are required to comply with the rules and regulations of the Securities Commission regarding issuing of prospectuses, etc.

3. Closely held (private) corporations

Obviously, not all corporations are incorporated for the purpose of selling shares and raising large amounts of capital from the public. The general advantages of incorporation were explained earlier. To give small businesses the advantage of incorporation, a different type of company was created by both provincial and federal legislation.

Private corporations can be more accurately described as "incorporated partnerships" rather than as corporations as we normally view them because they usually consist of one, two or three people who are close personal friends, business associates, or family members.

Another important distinction to be kept in mind is that in public corporations the directors, officers and shareholders are separate individuals.

In private corporations, each individual may hold two or three positions in the corporation. For example, it is not unusual for one person to be, at the same time, a shareholder, officer and director.

The directors on the board of a public corporation are usually a group of business people respected in the community who bring to the board a wide variety of business experience. Their function is to act as "watchdog" over the officers and to protect the shareholders' interests.

Most officers of large public corporations are "hired professionals" and they are in charge of the day-to-day activities. In many instances they also wield the greatest influence on the overall operations of the corporation.

Usually the two or three top officers of the corporation are also members of the board of directors.

The last group in a public corporation, but certainly the largest in terms of numbers, consists of the shareholders. In public corporations, this group is the theoretical "owner" of the corporation which, in turn, owns the assets. Shares represent ownership. However, ownership of shares does not usually vest in the shareholder the right or power to run the corporation.

In theory the final authority for a corporation's operations rests with the shareholders. In the reality of public corporations this concept is a myth for many reasons.

Shareholders are often spread all over the country, so very few attend the annual meeting. Most shareholders want only a return on their investment (dividends) and an increase in value of their shares; they do not want to run a company. If the corporation does not perform satisfactorily, the shareholders rarely call the management or directors to task or replace them. The shares are simply sold. Furthermore, many shareholders lack the competence and business experience necessary to run the business properly so they hesitate to question the activities of managing officers or directors.

The last reason, but not the least, is the fact that the usual wide dispersal of shareholders means that it will take a great deal of time, money and effort for a group of reform-minded individuals to obtain enough support to seriously challenge the management or directors of the corporation.

If you were to visualize the hierarchy of a public corporation, it would look like this:

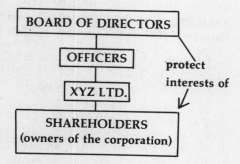

All corporations must have directors, officers, and shareholders. One distinction between public and private corporations is that in public companies these

positions are generally occupied by different persons.

A vice-president in a public corporation will not necessarily be on the board of directors, and will almost certainly not own enough shares of the corporation to affect corporate policy from a shareholder's position.

His or her effect on the operations of the corporation will derive solely from his or her position as an officer of the corporation.

In a private corporation, these positions are usually occupied by the same people. For example, if you have a "family" corporation where the husband has 50% of the shares, the wife 25%, and a son the other 25%, it is likely that these people will be the sole directors.

You need at least one director as well as two officers. Be careful not to confuse these positions, even though the people occupying them are the same. In a private corporation you are often wearing more than one hat at the same time.

To illustrate, in the day-to-day activities of your small business, you are wearing the hat of an officer. If you decide, however, to branch out into a new area, or to purchase or sell substantial assets, you are wearing the hat of a director. (Important matters which will have considerable effect on the corporation are usually referred to the board of directors.)

When you attend the annual meeting and vote on issues or buy or sell shares you are acting as a shareholder. The shareholder always has the final say on any serious issue because shareholdings represent ownership of the corporation.

You will find instances where "partners" in a business on a day-to-day level are not 50/50 owners of a corporation on a shareholding basis.

This is one of the great dangers of incorporating a small business. The minority shareholder (less than 50%) is usually in a precarious position with regard to the majority shareholder (more than 50%).

I suggest that if you're in an incorporated "partnership" with another person who is not related to you that you choose one of the following options.

(a) Each of you take say 49% of the shares and ask a trusted, knowledgeable business acquaintance to hold 2%. By doing this you will provide a mechanism for resolving disputes between you and your partner, or

(b) You take a chance and divide the shares 50/50.

(c) Prepare and execute a shareholders' agreement which contemplates the everyday management of the company.

You might ask what will happen when there is a basic disagreement over some issue and a deadlock results. The answer is that either the assets are sold and the business is wound up, or one party buys out the other.

This reflects the basic nature of a private corporation, which is that of an incorporated "partnership."

We all know what happens when partners in a business have an irreconcilable difference. The same is true in a small corporation. But a 50/50 split of the shares does encourage co-operation.

When this balance is altered it will, of necessity, affect the personal relationship of the "partners."

It is important to note that for the purpose of this book only the incorporation of a corporation that is not offering its securities to the public will be discussed.

The distinction between corporations that offer securities to the public and corporations that do not is important and must be continually borne in mind, particularly in the case of growing organizations seeking alternative methods of raising capital financing.

e. ONE-PERSON CORPORATIONS

The Business Corporations Act, 1982 allows the formation of a one-person corporation. This means that the same person may be all of the following: the president and secretary, sole director, and sole shareholder.

The evolution of one-person corporations recognizes that many persons are in business solely with and for themselves. (This is the so-called incorporated proprietorship.)

The procedures for incorporation are essentially the same for the one-person corporation as for the two-or-more-person corporation, but from a practical standpoint, the one-person corporation generally approves corporate transactions by passing a director's resolution, rather than conducting a meeting to do so (see chapter 5 for further details).

f. HOW MANY SHARES SHOULD YOU ISSUE?

A quick look ahead in the book at our model set of Articles of Incorporation will show that we have capitalized our corporation with an unlimited number of shares.

You will also note that out of this "pool" we have issued 10 shares to the incorporator, John Doe, for a price of $10 which should be deposited into the corporation's bank account.

You may ask: why only issue 10 shares when the total number of shares authorized is unlimited? There are a number of reasons.

After the new corporation is incorporated and organized, it will require financing in order to begin operations.

How does capital flow into a business? There are two methods:

(a) By investing in shares, i.e., equity capital

(b) By lending money to the business in some form or other, i.e., shareholder loans, bonds, debentures

There are some definite advantages to capitalizing a business through loans, as opposed to buying shares, especially a high-risk business such as a newly "incorporated partnership."

The first advantage is that capital "loaned" to the corporation, as opposed to "invested" in the corporation, can be repaid at any time tax-free, i.e., a loan to the corporation repaid to a shareholder is not income to the shareholder.

On the other hand, money invested in shares cannot be repaid while the corporation is operating; therefore, any withdrawal of capital by the owners is generally done through payment of wages or dividends which are taxable in the receiver's hands.

Second, if the new corporation is in financial difficulty, a shareholder loan ranks equally with the other creditors when dividing up the remainder of the assets, and ranks ahead of repayment to the shareholders for money invested in shares. Common shareholders rarely see any proceeds when a company goes bankrupt.

Another major reason for not using more shares is to keep the initial capital investment at a minimum.

As an alternative to issuing only 10 shares, you may want to consider issuing 1 000 shares at $0.10 per share. This way, it will be easier to sell any of these shares to another person, because each share will have a lower value than if only 10 shares were issued. Similarly, it will be easier for a newcomer to your company to subscribe for shares from the company treasury since each share would have a lower value than if only 10 shares had been issued initially.

Looking ahead, there is simply no advantage in financing the company by issuing shares only.

There is no real need in most simple incorporation situations to issue immediately all of the shares that you incorporated with to shareholders. The unissued shares remain in the company treasury and belong to the corporation itself until it becomes necessary to issue them to new shareholders. Just visualize all unissued shares as sitting in a large pot labelled "Company treasury" until directors' minutes issuing them to new shareholders are drawn up and filed in the minute book.

If a company is incorporated with an unlimited number of shares, and there are only two shareholders, then, for example, only 10 shares need to be issued to all the shareholders. If they each have an equal number of the issued shares their interests are the same as if they had each taken 5 000 of the corporation's shares.

A final and most important reason is that, if your business is successful, you may wish to bring in other "partners" who want to invest in the business. At that time a valuation of the amount of "equity" you have in the business will have to be made by your accountant.

Equity is defined as assets minus liabilities and represents the net worth of the business. From the examples here you can see that it makes no difference how many total shares are issued as long as your positon with regard to other shareholders is not altered. Also, by keeping most of the shares in the treasury, you will be flexible enough to meet new corporate developments.

Samples #4 and #5 are balance sheets for a corporation where the number of shares issued to shareholders is 10 and 10 000 respectively. I have purposely simplified matters by deducting shareholders' contributions in each case because this is like transferring money from one hand to the next in a small, nonpublic corporation. I have also deliberately ignored the "goodwill" or capitalization of earnings factor which merely serves to place a multiple factor on the net earnings.

As you can see in Samples #4 and #5, John Doe's business is worth the same on a net return basis.

Another common situation is where another shareholder is brought in. In such a case you have two alternatives to consider.

First, you may simply transfer a percentage of each of the existing shareholder's holdings to the new "partner." If the shares are sold for more than you paid for them you will have to think about the capital gains tax liability.

Another problem with this method is that frequently you end up with a fractional share situation which is always annoying to deal with, to say the least.

For example, suppose we had John and Jack Doe each owning 50 shares. Say their cousin Helen becomes involved and all parties agree that she should be an equal shareholder. In order to do this, both Jack and John would have to transfer 16 2/3 shares to Helen and each party would be left with 33 1/3 shares which is an awkward situation.

A better solution would be to issue 25 more shares each to John and Jack Doe and then transfer them to Helen. Again, capital gains tax would have to be considered if the shares are transferred at a higher price than they were issued for.

If, on the other hand, the shares were issued at, say $5 per share and this amount was paid into the company and the shares were then transferred for the same amount, then no tax would be payable.

The other alternative is to issue additional shares directly from treasury to Helen at the price agreed upon. In this case no capital gains tax would be payable because the money simply flows into the capital account of the corporation.

Of course, there would also be no direct benefit to John and Jack in bringing Helen in, other than her contribution to the work effort.

In other words, the corporation would have additional funds with which to finance its activities, but Jack and John could not receive any financial benefit from Helen's purchase without paying tax.

In most cases, then, it is simpler to issue additional shares, either directly to the new shareholder, or to the existing members first and then transfer them to the new partner, rather than get involved in complicated partial share arrangements.

To recap briefly, since there is no particular advantage to issuing all the shares unless you are involved in a complicated share control problem, and there are several disadvantages to capitalizing through share capital, it is wise to issue a minimum to begin with, say 100 to 1 000 to each shareholder depending on the number of persons involved.

I have already covered the advantages of financing the corporation through loans rather than equity. You lend the corporation capital by simply writing a cheque and making a note on the cheque and bank deposit slip that it is a shareholder's loan. You can further record the fact that it is a shareholder's loan by drawing up directors' minutes and a promissory or demand note for its repayment. (See the chapter on post-incorporation procedures.) Your accountant or bookkeeper can make the proper entries from your cheque stubs.

g. CLASSES OF SHARES

As most small private corporations have no need for many different classes of shares, do-it-yourselfers may ignore this section unless you are curious.

Generally speaking, shares can have innumerable rights and restrictions attached to them. A class of shares then can be any set of shares which have attached to them rights different from the rights attached to another set of shares.

For example, when you start your business, you, like most people, should incorporate with and issue "common

SAMPLE #4
BALANCE SHEET
(where 10 shares are issued)

JOHN DOE & ASSOCIATES LTD.

ASSETS		LIABILITIES	
Cash	$ 10	Note to the bank	$2 000
Inventory	4 000	Shareholder loan	3 000
Building	5 000		
Total assets	$9 010	Total liability	$5 000

NET WORTH

Capital stock authorized — unlimited shares	
Issued 10 shares at $1.00 each	$ 10
Retained earnings	4 000
Total liability and equity	$9 010

Note: The corporation has earned $4 000 to date. Each share is worth $401 (total net worth divided by 10) but as $1 of this amount is shareholders' money and it is really a matter of transferring it from one hand to the other, it really should not be included in determining the value of the corporation from the shareholder's point of view. Therefore, if the assets of the corporation were liquidated tomorrow it would be worth $4 000 in *net return* to the shareholders.

shares" to all of the incorporators, so that all the shareholders of the corporation have equal rights to vote and receive dividends. When your corporation becomes successful, you might wish to create a different class of shares which, when issued to shareholders, will give them the right to receive dividends before holders of any other class of shares, or which have cumulative dividend rights, or rights to be redeemed by the corporation. You might refer to the new class of shares as "preferred" shares in order to distinguish them from the other shares that you first issued from the treasury pool. Large public corporations usually have different classes of shares.

Remember, it is much easier to add rights and restrictions at a later date rather than attach them now and then have to buy them up or strip them. If, at a later date, you wish to create classes of shares that have different rights attached to them, you should see a lawyer so you can carry out the alterations of your Articles correctly and design your capital structure properly to minimize taxes and maximize control.

SAMPLE #5
BALANCE SHEET
(where 10 000 shares issued)

JOHN DOE & ASSOCIATES LTD.

ASSETS		LIABILITIES	
Cash	$40 000	Note to the bank	$2 000
Inventory	4 000	Shareholder loan	3 000
Building	5 000		
Total assets	$49 000	Total liability	$5 000

NET WORTH

Capital stock authorized — unlimited shares	
Issued 10 000 shares at $4.00 each to John Doe	$40 000
Retained earnings	4 000
Total liabilities and equity	$49 000

Note: If the business is wound up, John Doe's shares are worth $44 000 but $40 000 of this is John Doe's own money. Therefore, the net return would again be $4 000.

14

2

TAX ADVANTAGES TO INCORPORATING

There can be substantial tax advantages to incorporating your business. This section outlines the major ones.

a. BASIC CORPORATE RATE*

The basic combined federal and provincial corporate income tax rate before the small business deduction and manufacturing and processing credit is currently approximately 48%. The rate on income from manufacturing operations is about 43%. The rate on manufacturing income will be reduced to 38% by July 1, 1991.

b. QUALIFYING FOR THE SMALL BUSINESS TAX RATE*

Provided your business can qualify for the small business rate, there is a substantial reduction in taxes payable on business earnings. Effective July 1, 1988, the rate for the first $200 000 of all net income from active business is about 22%.

There is a corporate provincial tax holiday in Ontario for small business corporations that can reduce the rate to as little as 12%. It is a three-year tax holiday for newly formed small business corporations.

To qualify for the small business rate on the first $200 000 of net income from an *active* business, there are two basic tests to meet:

(a) Your corporation must be a Canadian-controlled private corporation; that is, a private Canadian corporation other than a corporation controlled directly or indirectly by one or more non-residents or by one or more public corporations or by any such combination.

(b) Your company must generate income from an *active* business in Canada to be eligible for the small business rate.

If the corporation fails both tests, then the tax rate will be between approximately 43% and 49% depending on whether the income is from manufacturing and processing or not.

Any business carried on by your corporation will be considered active with two exceptions: personal services businesses (which refers to personal services that would ordinarily be provided by an individual employee rather than by a company) and investment businesses. Companies that carry on these two kinds of business will be taxed at the top corporate rate. Furthermore, a company carrying on a personal services business (sometimes referred to as an "incorporated employee") will not be allowed all the deductions available to other companies.

These two exceptions to the active business rules will not, however, apply if the company has six or more full-time employees throughout the year or in the case of a management service company, it receives its income from a corporation associated with it. In such cases, investment companies and "incorporated employees" will both be eligible for the low tax rate.

Assuming you qualify for the small business rate, the tax advantages to incorporating are outlined below.

c. MINIMIZE NON-DEDUCTIBLE OR DEPRECIABLE EXPENSES

First, you realize an immediate tax savings by doing it yourself, and this is over

* All rates depend on the province in which you reside and whether the provincial corporate rates remain as they are.

and above the straight cost savings. This is because lawyer's and Registrar's fees for incorporation are not wholly tax deductible as an expense. (They are deductible only to the extent of 50% of the expenditure on a 10% declining balance basis.)

d. SPLIT YOUR INCOME

Second, with a company, you can effectively "split" your income. For example, say your business made $75 000 last year as a proprietorship. This entire amount would be considered your personal income and be taxed on an ascending scale up to about 46%.*

On the other hand, if you have incorporated, $25 000 could be paid to you personally as salary or bonus and $50 000 could be left in the company. This $50 000 would be taxed at the rate of 22% *if* your company qualifies for the small business tax rate.

On the $25 000 paid out to you personally, you would pay tax in the 8% to 32% range, depending on the number of personal deductions, etc. you have. The top personal marginal rate will be between 42% and 52% depending on the province you live in.

This is just one example. In fact, you are allowed to work out any combination that keeps your total tax bill to a minimum, including employing members of your family, provided they are employed in a bona fide capacity and the payment is reasonable.

Currently, a qualifying company's tax rate is only 22% on all earnings below $200 000 in each year. Therefore, if your company's earnings are $50 000 a year, you will pay only 22% in taxes each year.

A further split is also possible. After paying this initial corporate tax, you can then choose to either leave the funds in the company or pay out dividends to the shareholders (you, your spouse, and children).

Depending upon other sources of income and your personal income tax bracket, it may be more advantageous for one or more of your family members to take payments from the company in the form of dividends alone or in a mixture of dividends and salary. An individual (other than a resident of Quebec), with no other sources of income will be able to receive approximately $22 000 of Canadian dividends in 1989 without being subject to tax. This is because of the dividend tax credit. However, the company must be carefully structured for this technique to work properly.

However, since dividends are not deductible and it is important to limit, if at all possible, net corporate business income to $200 000 in order to pay the lowest corporate income tax rate, payments of bonuses and salary may be preferable to dividends.

One critical point to keep in mind is that dividend income does *not* qualify as "earned income" for purposes of making a deductible contribution to an RRSP. Thus, if your entire income consisted of dividends, you could not get a deduction for any contribution to your RRSP. Furthermore, your income might also be subject to the new minimum tax.

e. ESTATE PLANNING BENEFITS

With a company, you can effect substantial estate planning advantages. As this is a technical area and beyond the scope of this book, it will not be discussed at any length. Suffice it to say that the existence of a company enables you to own a widely diversified portfolio of assets (including all kinds of property) under the ownership of a single entity.

This can be a great advantage both from a tax and administrative point of view, especially if the company is located in a jurisdiction like Ontario which does not have estate taxes, and the assets are located in a jurisdiction that does.

* Effective January 1, 1988, this rate may be greater or less depending on the province in which you reside.

f. USE SALARY AND BONUS ACCRUALS

Through a company, you can declare yourself a bonus that is deductible from the company's income but need not be declared by you as income until it is actually paid. However, the Income Tax Act has rules about how long you can delay declaring the payment as income to you. The rules say that the bonus has to be taken within 180 days from the end of your corporation's tax year in which the bonus was declared. For example, if your company's year end was January 31 and you declared yourself a bonus of $10 000 on January 30, 1989, the company would deduct it as a salary expense for the 1988-89 year only if the bonus was actually paid by July 31, 1989. The result is that you would pay personal tax on the bonus in April, 1990 (less, of course, the tax the company would have to withhold when it paid you the bonus).

You can see that this gives you some flexibility. To be deductible these bonuses must be reasonable (in relation to services rendered to the company) and represent a legal liability of the company. (Passing a directors' resolution is advisable.)

In addition, there are other tax wrinkles and elections relating to the salary/dividend/bonus route which any competent tax advisor can tell you about.

The important thing to remember is that you must be careful in planning bonuses to look at the overall tax liability of your company *and* you. If your company is already able to take advantage of the low small business tax rate, there is little sense in declaring a bonus that will be taxed in your hands as income at a slightly higher rate.

If you want to reduce your company's earnings so that it can take advantage of the small business rate, you might want to declare a bonus payable to yourself, and wait before paying it to yourself (but no longer than six months after year end). In this way you can "even out" the earnings and so pay less total tax over a period of years. For example, if you can foresee that your company's earnings for the fiscal year will exceed the amount eligible for the small business tax rate, declare a bonus for yourself as it may reduce the earnings sufficiently to enable the company to be taxed at the lower small business rate, or mean less money is taxable at a higher rate.

Furthermore, by reducing your corporate profits you reduce the size of the tax instalment payments payable by the corporation and, therefore, improve your cash flow position.

If you declare dividends payable to yourself, there is no time limit on when they can be paid to you. Once the corporation has paid tax on its profits, dividends can be distributed at any time. This might be beneficial from the point of view of liability for personal income tax.

Remember, whichever method you choose to distribute your corporate earnings, it must be designed to meet the monetary needs and tax liability of both you and the company.

g. EXPENSE DEDUCTIONS

Aside from the fact that operating your business through a limited company *may* allow you to claim more liberal entertainment and travel expenses, there are perfectly legal and sanctioned ways of using a company to increase expense allowances.

For example, country club and similar dues paid by your company on your behalf, while not tax deductible by the company, do not have to be included in your personal income, provided you use the clubs for business entertainment. Therefore, because the company is taxed at a lower rate than you are personally, it can earn less than you personally to net the same amount.

However, the case of business meals and entertainment will only be deductible to the extent of 80% of their cost. The cost of business meals and entertainment subject to the 80% limitation includes gratuities, overcharges, room rentals at a hotel to provide entertainment, and tickets for various entertainment events.

Similarly, if you are arranging life insurance policies, the company can pay the premiums (non-deductible — but the money earned to pay the premium is taxed at a lower rate) and any proceeds collected by the company are non-taxable.

h. PLANNING FOR YOUR RETIREMENT

In the past, the opportunity for small business owners to provide for their own retirement was exceptional. Unfortunately, that is no longer the case.

If you are an owner/employee of a corporation, you may not be a beneficiary of your corporation's DPSP. If the company does not have a deferred profit-sharing plan (DPSP) or a registered pension plan (RPP), or you are not a beneficiary, your maximum contribution to a registered retirement savings plan can be $7 500 or 20% of your earned income, whichever is less.

Draft legislation released March 28, 1988 and the Information Release issued by the Department of Finance on August 19, 1988 would delay the phasing in of higher RRSP contribution limits until 1995. Although the final legislation may differ from the draft legislation and the changes thereto announced in the Information Release, under pension reform your RRSP dollar limits will likely increase over time for an individual who is not a member of a DPSP or an RPP and are as follows:

1989 — $ 9 500
1990 — $11 500
1991 — $13 500
1992 — $15 500

Retiring allowances given to employees or employee/shareholders can be transferred to an RRSP, but are limited to $3 500 for each year the employee did not have vested rights under an RPP or

DPSP, and $2 000 for each year the employee did have such vested benefits. Under pension reform, proposals for years of service commencing in 1989, the transfer would be limited to $2 000 per year of service.

i. INTEREST-FREE AND LOW-INTEREST LOANS TO EMPLOYEES AND SHAREHOLDERS

In the past, companies could make low- or no-interest loans to employees without creating a taxable benefit. This was especially valuable where the employee-shareholder was using the loan to —

(a) build a home,
(b) relocate and buy a home at least 25 miles closer to the work place,
(c) purchase shares in the company, or
(d) buy a car for use in his or her duties as an employee.

In 1981 these benefits were made fully taxable. As a result, loans made to employees attract "imputed" interest income to the employee if made interest-free or below the "prescribed" loan rate set by the government (currently 9%). This rate is adjusted quarterly based on the interest rate paid on 91-day treasury bills for the previous quarter. In other words, on a no-interest loan of $10 000, $900 is added to employees' income.

However, on loans to purchase shares in their employer company, employees will be able to deduct the interest expense against all other employment income or income from property and dividends provided the shares bought are either preferred shares that yield taxable dividends higher than the prescribed interest rate, or common shares. Thus, no net benefit will be included in the employee's income. It should be noted, however, that commencing January 1, 1988 to the extent that an employee's interest expense exceeds income from property (e.g., interest and dividends, etc.) it will effectively reduce any immediate access to the capital gains exemption by the amount of such excess until such excess is ultimately absorbed by income from property.

However, where the loan is made to allow the employee to buy a car to be used on the job, the maximum deduction for interest costs is $250 per month. However, in order to deduct this maximum interest amount you must drive your car no less than 24 000 kilometres per year. Commencing January 1, 1988 there are very complex rules pertaining to the deduction of automobile expenses and your professional advisors should be consulted.

To summarize, low-interest or no-interest bearing loans to employees are no longer as beneficial as they once were unless they are made to allow the employee to buy shares of the employer company. Loans to allow an employee to buy a car can also be beneficial, but not to the same extent as share purchase loans.

j. MANUFACTURING AND PROCESSING CREDIT (M&P)

All active small business income will be taxed at the same rate from July 1, 1988 and the rates on such income will range from about 12% to 22% depending on the province in which your company resides. For income not eligible for the small business rate, the M&P credit will be reduced to 2% from July 1, 1988 and will then increase by 1% each July 1 after, to a maximum of 5% for 1991 and subsequent taxation years, with the result that in 1991 the rate of tax on manufacturing income not eligible for the small business rate will range from about 26% to 40% depending on the province in which your company resides.

The M&P credit was introduced to reward labor intensive businesses, supposedly as a stimulus to employment. The Income Tax Act specifically *excludes* certain activities from qualifying. They are farming, fishing, logging, on-site job construction, most natural resource activities; and

any manufacturing endeavor where manufacturing revenues are less than 10% of the gross sales.

The important thing here is that there are a lot of businesses that qualify that you wouldn't normally think would. For example, newspapers or any type of printing business would qualify. In fact, any business that changes, converts, adds to, or re-assembles the raw material may qualify.

If your business is primarily manufacturing and processing in Canada, did not carry on active business outside the country in the year, and did not carry on activities specifically excluded from the definition of manufacturing and processing, all of your company's income qualifies for this credit so long as its income does not exceed $22 000.

k. ANTI-AVOIDANCE

The federal Minister of Finance has introduced a new general anti-avoidance rule. Any transaction that results in a significant reduction or even deferral of the tax that might have been payable had the transaction not occurred can be completely ignored unless it can be shown to have had a bona fide non-tax purpose.

l. CONCLUSION

The realization that profits mean taxes tends to cause business people to over-react and become more and more committed to minimizing their tax load. This is totally understandable and perfectly acceptable, as long as the methods used do not cause the tax tail to wag the dog and are legal.

The best way of achieving the lowest possible taxes is to maintain proper and accurate records and ensure that you have at your disposal the legal and accounting expertise you require to assist you in taking advantage of all of the opportunities available under the current tax laws.

3

INCORPORATION PROCEDURE FOR AN ONTARIO CORPORATION NOT OFFERING ITS SECURITIES TO THE PUBLIC

a. SUMMARY OF PROCEDURES

Every person incorporating a corporation should purchase the latest edition of The Business Corporations Act, 1982. While many acts are difficult to understand, the Business Corporations Act, 1982 is clearly written and is well indexed and organized. It may be purchased from the Queen's Printer (provincial government) in Toronto.

For other pertinent information of a preliminary nature contact:

Ministry of Consumer and
    Commercial Relations
393 University Avenue
Toronto, Ontario
M7A 2H6
Hours: 8:00 a.m. to 4:30 p.m., Monday through Friday.

The fee which must accompany any application for incorporation may be found in the Schedule to the Regulations at the end of the Business Corporations Act, 1982.

The section applicable to incorporating fees is reproduced in Table #1.

TABLE #1
SCHEDULE OF FEES

Filing articles of incorporation and endorsing a certificate	$250
Filing and issue of certificate for restated articles of incorporation	$100
Filing and issue of certificate for Articles of Amendment	$100
Filing articles of arrangement, and endorsing a certificate	$250
Application for order permitting corporate records to be kept elsewhere than at the registered office under subsection 144(3)	$100
Rescission of order regarding corporate records under subsection 144(4)	$20
Filing articles of revival, and endorsing a certificate	$250

The following is a general, abbreviated, step-by-step list of the procedures necessary to incorporate a business corporation in Ontario.

Each of these steps will be discussed in detail in the sections of the book following.

(a) Select a name and submit it to a name search firm.

(b) Once your name is approved, complete and file —
   (i) duplicate copies of the Articles of Incorporation,
   (ii) any needed consent forms,
   (iii) any name search forms forwarded to you by a name search company.

(c) Send all of the above to the Director, Companies Branch, along with a certified cheque for incorporation fees payable to the Treasurer, Ontario.

(d) When approved, the Director will issue a Certificate of Incorporation and return to you a certified copy of the Articles. He will also publish the appropriate notice in the Ontario *Gazette*.

(e) Purchase a minute book, share certificates and company seal.

(f) Make banking arrangements with your bank.

(g) Prepare organizational resolutions of directors and shareholders including the banking resolutions.

(h) Insert Certificate of Incorporation, by-laws and resolutions of shareholders and directors in the minute book.

(i) Issue share certificates.

(j) Complete registers in minute book.

b. CHOOSING A NAME

A corporation, like a person, must have a name, but unfortunately it is not as easy to pick a name for a corporation as it is for a new baby. When you select a name for your corporation, you must consider certain definite factors, the most important one being that the name must be acceptable to the Director, Companies Branch. In broad terms, the Director will approve any name which is not identical to, or closely resembles, any existing corporation names. Names that are similar to existing names may be rejected because they will possibly be confused in the minds of the public.

You are responsible for selecting a name that complies with the act and that you are entitled to use. You do not want to be required at some later date to change your name.

With this in mind you should try for one that is distinctive and accurately describes the type of business that you intend to carry on. For example, a name like "Quiggly Cleaners Ltd." would be a better name for a drycleaning company than "Eastern Enterprises Ltd." The word "Eastern" is one of those words that has been so frequently used in names that it is no longer distinctive. Other words that have met the same fate are "Northern," "Pacific," "Universal," "Maple Leaf," and a host of others that I am sure you can think of. The word "enterprises" does not describe the business of this particular company, although it might be used accurately in naming an investment company of some sort.

One of the easiest ways to check out existing names is to look in the yellow pages for the names of corporations already doing business in your area. Trade and corporation directories which are available in any large library will help you find other protected names of Canadian organizations.

Generally, you should remember that the most successful proposals are likely to be —

(a) a coined word (perhaps a combination of incorporators' names) plus a descriptive word,

(b) the full name of an individual (e.g., John Albert Doe Ltd.),

(c) the name of an individual combined with a descriptive word, (e.g., Doe Explorations Ltd.), or

(d) the combination of a distinctive geographic name plus a descriptive word (e.g., Niagara Machine Works Ltd.) provided the company is connected with or operating in that area.

Of course, all proposals must end with the words "Limited," "Limitée," "Incorporated," "Incorporée," "Corporation" or the abbreviation of these words.

You can set out your company name in an English form, a French form, an English form and a French form, or a combined English and French form, and it may be legally designated by any such name.

Only letters from the English alphabet or Arabic numerals or combination thereof, together with the necessary punctuation marks, may form part of the company name.

In selecting your name, you should avoid using words like "Institute," "Condominium," or "Co-operative" which are restricted to specific organizations in many provinces.

Furthermore, you should not use any names which imply a connection with or approval of the Royal Family. Names using words like "Imperial" or "Royal" will be rejected. Finally, names that imply government approval or the sponsorship of a branch, service, or department are frequently not acceptable. That eliminates words like "Parliament Hill," "R.C.M.P.," and "legislative" from the list of choices.

In addition, you should know that you may not receive approval for a name that could possibly be construed as obscene or that is too general in that it only describes the quality, goods or function of the services. Companies with names like "General Motors" and "Best Foods" have more or less taken up these choices.

Stay away from the names of companies already in existence (or the common contractions of their names). For example, a name like Xerox Construction Ltd. implies that your resources are connected with those of Xerox. This is okay if you can show that it is true. If it is not, you may be found liable of trying to "steal" the name in a "passing off" action brought by Xerox. You may also get into trouble, or at the very least have your choice rejected if it is a name like Inco Investments Ltd. The word "Inco" is a commonly used contraction for the International Nickel Company of Canada Ltd.

While you might think it is easier and more prestigious to give your corporation your own name there are a few pitfalls that you should be aware of.

If you decide to sell your corporation, your name, with its goodwill and business reputation, goes with it to the new owner, unless, of course, you want to take a considerable loss on the sale price. Suppose the new owner doesn't have your head for business and the company with your name on it goes bankrupt. You may have some embarrassing moments when people first meet you and inquire whether or not you are *the* John Doe who went bankrupt a few years ago while owing their brother-in-law $10 000. It is a small world and people have long memories for this sort of thing.

A further disadvantage to using your own name for a corporation dealing with the public is that people cannot immediately tell what type of business you are in so potential customers may be deterred. Corporations that intend to rely on the general public for business (as opposed to family holding corporations) should have a name which informs the public of the goods or services they offer.

Customer resistence to the idea of doing business with a "large, impersonal corporation" can be overcome by good service, and an appealing corporate name. You may wish to seek professional advice from name search companies that assist in selecting a company name.

It might be noted that as a general rule the name of an individual, such as John Doe Inc., will be granted provided it is not similar to an existing corporate name and John Doe's consent accompanies the application.

For example, in this case, if you are John Doe, you simply complete the form shown as Sample #12 which is included in the package of forms available from the publisher.

c. CHECKING YOUR NAME

Before you submit your incorporating documents, you should first have your name checked by an Ontario name search firm.

The Companies Branch does not search and reserve proposed names. It is your responsibility to get a name search report from a private search company, decide on the availability of your proposed name, and ensure that your articles meet the requirements of the act.

If the name is unimportant to you, or if you really are in a hurry to incorporate, you can submit your documents with a blank space for the name followed by the words, "Ontario Limited" and the Companies Branch will assign a number name to your corporation.

In most instances you will want a name that is pleasing to the public, so you would be wiser to check out names and choose the one that is available. Take some care in making your choice as in order to amend your corporation's name, you must follow a special procedure set out in the act and pay additional fees.

The proposed name, or preferably three proposed names, in order of your preference should be submitted to a name search firm in a letter. An example of such a letter appears in Sample #6.

The name search corporations use their own computer terminals to scan the information contained in computers operated by the federal and Ontario governments concerning business and corporate names. They charge a fee of approximately $40 to $50 for each name search, which must be paid for in advance by certified cheque. They will send you a form (see Sample #7) and a four-page computer printout listing existing corporations with similar names. Both these forms must be sent to the Companies Branch with your articles.

While the computer print-out will assist you in determining that your corporate name is not the same as or similar to another company, it does not guarantee that your name is protected from any future proceedings. After you have incorporated, if it is determined that the name you selected *is* similar to another name, you may be required to change your company name.

Furthermore, the protection afforded to your company name upon incorporation extends only throughout Ontario. If you are considering doing business across Canada, you should seek professional advice as to the merits of trade mark protection, or incorporation as a federal company. See *Federal Incorporation and Business Guide*, another Self-Counsel title.

Finally, you must file your Articles of Incorporation along with your print-out within 90 days of doing your name search and receiving the print-out.

The name search corporation must use the NUANS system for computer reports.

For a free brochure or further information concerning the services offered by these corporations you may contact them at the addresses listed here.

TORONTO

ABC Name Search & Reservations Ltd.
1 St. Johns Road
Brampton, Ontario
L6T 3Z8
Telephone: (416) 794-0203

CCNS Corporate Services Ltd.
393 University Avenue
Suite 2010
Toronto, Ontario
M5G 1E6
Telephone: (416) 977-6530
Zenith: 1-800-268-8301
Telex: 06-217802

Dye & Durham Co. Limited
160 Bartley Drive
Toronto, Ontario
M4A 1E2
Telephone: (416) 751-9644

Finders Research
202-111 Elizabeth Street
Toronto, Ontario
M5G 1P7
Telephone: (416) 599-9472

Idealogic Corporation
Idealogic Searchhouse Division
50 Richmond Street
Toronto, Ontario
M5C 1X9
Telephone: (416) 863-9747

International Tradename
   Clearance Inc.
2 Carlton Street
Suite 808
Toronto, Ontario
M5B 1J3
Telephone: (416) 977-0522
Toll-free 1-800-268-8036 or
          1-800-268-8086

Incorporators Unlimited
2 Gloucester Street
Suite 203
Toronto, Ontario
M4Y 1L5
Telephone: (416) 968-0865

Kam Computer Applications Inc.
593 Yonge Street
Suite 212
Toronto, Ontario
M4Y 1Z4
Telephone: (416) 923-1231

National Corporate Name Clearance
   Corp. (NCI)
730 Yonge Street
Suite 204
Toronto, Ontario
M4Y 2B7
Telephone: (416) 923-4080
Zenith: 1-800-268-7580

Newsome and Gilbert, Limited
Incorporation Services
177 Front Street E.
Toronto, Ontario
M5A 3S2
Telephone: (416) 363-7061 or
1-800-268-8106

LONDON
Documat Legal Search
45 King Street
London, Ontario
N6A 1B8
Telephone: (519) 673-3295
                679-9032

OTTAWA
Automated Legal Support Services
   Limited
350 Sparks Street
Suite 806
Ottawa, Ontario
K1R 7S8
Telephone: (613) 238-1519

House of Selective Researchers Inc./
Maison de Recherches Selectives Inc.
307 - 150 Metcalfe Street
Ottawa, Ontario
K2P 1P1
Telephone: (613) 236-3841

SAMPLE #6
LETTER TO NAME SEARCH CORPORATION

January 7, 198-

Nameless Name Searchers
111 Founders Lane
Anytown, Ontario

Dear Director:

Re: John Doe & Associates Limited   1
John Doe's Personnel Incorporated   2
J. D. Personnel Corporation   3

We wish to incorporate a company under one of the above names, which are listed in order of our preference. Please do the required search, and report to us.

Enclosed is a certified cheque for $ _____ .

Yours very truly,

John A. Doe
_____

SAMPLE #7
NAME SEARCH FORM

ONTARIO NAME SEARCH FORM

DATE: Oct. 3/198-   SEARCH NO.

AGENT:

☐ Name   ☐ Name   ☐
  Search   Reservation

FIRM: THE LAW SHOPPE
                                                          979-0000

REQUESTED BY: LORRAINE
                                                          TORONTO

Proposed Name: CLARI   ICE CREAM & CANDY LTD.

Nature of
Business:

Derivation   ☐ Coined   ☐ Person's   ☐ Place
of Key Word   Word   Name   Name
                ☐ Dictionary   ☐ Foreign Word
                  Word   Language & Meaning:

Consent of other

individual, body

corporate or firm

Proposed Name   ☐ Incorporation ☐ Extra Provincial ☐ Change
                  with Capital   Licence   of Name*

                ☐ Incorporation ☐
                  without Capital

*Give Present Name

Reservation   ☐ Please Reserve if Cleared

Second Choice: TON LTD.

Third Choice: GIE'S ICE CREAM & CANDY LTD.

PLEASE NOTE: Both this form and the computer printout bearing the Ontario Companies Branch clearance stamp, must accompany the articles application. Although we endeavor to ensure accuracy, we cannot assume responsbility for any errors or omissions.

PLEASE SEE REVERSE SIDE FOR CONDITIONS AND ADDITIONAL REQUIREMENTS

SAMPLE #8
COMPUTER PRINTOUT

```
CCA CANADA, NUANS-CC                                   NCNC    AE14170
                   ? CLARI        ICE CREAM                     PAGE 1
    1321464 ONTARIO                                             79/10/03

 98
    1321464 ONTARIO        CLARI      ICE CREAM
                                                                79/10/02
 NCNC       PROPOSED
 80
 0 261507 ONT             CHALET GLACE ICE CREAM
 CERTIF. OLDAMALG                                   LIMITED     72/10/04
 77
 35983576 P.Q.            CREME GLACEE CASCADE
                                                      INC       77/05/25 1


    18292912 ALTA         LANGHOLM CARRI
                                                      LTD       75/05/16 1

 76
 0 415049 ONT            DJS ICE CREAM PARLOURS
 CERTIF.                                           LIMITED      79/05/08
 LONDON ONT   N6C 2Y9              790530         0

    18810812 ALTA        CLARES      RIDGE RIDERS
                                                                66/03/14 1

 75
 0  35343 ONT            IDEAL ICE CREAM
 REMOVED                                           LIMITED      31/08/04

 0 338734 ONT            CLAUDIUS CARNEGIE ENTERPRISES CO
 CERTIF.                                             LTD        76/07/26
 74
 RN 44862 CANADA         CLAMDIGGERS
   ADQS.                                            TM-REGD     52/12/04

    31920523 P.Q.        ALASKA ICE CREAM
                                                     INC        74/01/04 1


 0 107536 ONT            ST. CLAIR ICE CREAM
                                                   LIMITED      60/06/30

 AN370751 CANADA         REGATTA ICE CREAM
   ACPU.                                            TM-APPL     73/12/11
 73      .
 0   36526 ONT           H. M. CLARIDGE INVESTMENTS
                                                   LIMITED      32/07/13

 0 410203 ONT            LA GONDOLA ICE CREAM
 CERTIF.                                             LTD        79/03/07
 TORONTO ONT   M4Y 1Y3             790328         0

    410203 ONT           LA GONDOLA ICE CREAM
                                                                79/03/07 1

 72
 0 242500 ONT            CARDER KLIMOWSKI CANADA
 CERTIF.                                            LIMITED     71/04/28

  B 420789 CANADA        EDS ICE CREAM PARLOUR
 RESTAURANT SERVICES, NAMELY                        TM-APPL     78/02/09
 58.                        '
```

Many businesses have a trade name that is different from the name of their corporation. The main reason for this is that the trade name is more easily remembered and is more effective for advertising purposes.

If you have registered, and you use, a name other than your corporate name, you are required to use the corporate name on all contracts, invoices, negotiable instruments and orders for goods or services.

If you are contemplating doing business under a name that is different from the name of your corporation, you should be aware of section 2 of the Corporations Information Act which provides as follows:

Chapter 96   CORPORATIONS INFORMATION   1980

Registration of business names

2. (1) No corporation shall carry on business in Ontario or identify itself to the public in Ontario by a name or style other than its corporate name unless the name or style is first registered with the Minister.

Idem

(2) A corporation may register a name or style referred to in subsection 1 by filing with the Minister a statement setting out,

(a) the name of the corporation;

(b) the jurisdiction in which it was incorporated;

(c) the name or style in which it intends to carry on business or identify itself to the public;

(d) a brief description of the business, activity or service to be carried on in or identified by the name being registered; and

(e) the location of its head office giving street and number, if any.

Idem

(3) The registration of a name or style under this section does not confer on the corporation any right to such name or style that it does not otherwise have.

Expiration and renewals

(4) Every registration made under this section expires in five years after the date of the registration, subject to renewal for a further period of five years from time to time.

You can pick up or order the Statement of Name Registration at 393 University Avenue, Toronto. It will cost you $50 to register it and should be done at the same time you are incorporating.

Sample #9 is an example of the statement referred to in sub-section (2).

This form is to be sent in together with your Articles of Incorporation, etc., to the Companies Branch.

STATEMENT OF NAME REGISTRATION

1978	1979	1980	1981	1982	1983	1984	1985	1986

Ministry of
Consumer and
Commercial
Ontario Relations

**REGISTRATION
OR
RENEWAL
OF
BUSINESS
NAME OR STYLE**
THE
CORPORATIONS
INFORMATION
ACT. 1976.
CD. 441

THIS REGISTRATION EXPIRES IN FIVE YEARS BUT MAY BE RENEWED. RENEWAL IS YOUR RESPONSIBILITY THE REGISTRATION EXPIRY DATE WILL BE SHOWN IN YOUR CERTIFICATE OF REGISTRATION. THE REGISTRATION DOES NOT CONFER ON THE CORPORATION ANY RIGHT TO THE NAME OR STYLE THAT IT DOES NOT OTHERWISE HAVE.

07197

1. NAME OR STYLE TO BE REGISTERED

Jolly John's Personnel Services

2. BUSINESS ACTIVITY OR SERVICE TO BE CARRIED ON IN OR IDENTIFIED BY THE REGISTERED NAME

Providing personnel services of any and all kinds and, without limiting the generality of the foregoing, to provide personnel management, planning, selection, placement and development

3. HEAD OFFICE LOCATION OF THE CORPORATION, GIVING STREET AND NUMBER OR R.R. NUMBER, MUNICIPALITY OR POST OFFICE AND PROVINCE

Suite 5600
390 Bay Street
Toronto, Ontario Z1P 0G0

4. INCORPORATING JURISDICTION

Ontario

5. ONTARIO CORPORATION NUMBER

2222222

6. NAME OF THE CORPORATION

John Doe & Associates

7. MAILING ADDRESS OF THE CORPORATION

Suite 5600
390 Bay Street, Toronto, Ontario Z1P 0G0

8. SIGNATURE OF DIRECTOR OR OFFICER

John Doe

9. NAME AND TITLE OF THE SIGNING OFFICIAL

President and Director
John Doe

MINISTRY USE ONLY

REGISTRATION DATE:

EXPIRY DATE

NOTWITHSTANDING THIS REGISTRATION THE CORPORATION MUST USE ITS CORPORATE NAME ON ALL CONTRACTS, INVOICES, NEGOTIABLE INSTRUMENTS AND ORDERS FOR GOODS OR SERVICES ISSUED OR MADE BY OR ON BEHALF OF THE CORPORATION.

SEE SECTION 2(4) OF THE CORPORATIONS INFORMATION ACT 1976.

INSTRUCTIONS AND DEFICIENCY NOTICE ON REVERSE SIDE

d. DRAFTING THE ARTICLES OF INCORPORATION

Application for the incorporation of a corporation in Ontario, excluding special types of corporations such as insurance companies, loan and trust companies, corporations without share capital (usually charitable and non-profit organizations), credit unions, co-operatives, finance and acceptance companies, is made by submitting duplicate, signed, dated and sworn copies of Articles of Incorporation to the Companies Division.

If the articles conform to law and are accompanied by the necessary approvals, they will be filed by the Minister, who will issue a Certificate of Incorporation. The certificate effectively begins the existence of the corporation as of the date set out on the certificate.

Articles of Incorporation may be submitted by one or more persons who must be 18 years of age or over, not of unsound mind or bankrupt, or by another corporation.

A corporation must also have one or more directors, who must be 18 years of age or over and not disqualified by the provisions of the act.

The Companies Branch provides instructions for use in submitting Articles of Incorporation. The forms may be obtained from one of your local stationers or they come as part of a package of forms that may be purchased, at nominal cost, from the publisher (see order form at front of book).

Sample #10 is a copy of the Articles of Incorporation for a service corporation — in this case, a personnel agency having one director.

It is incorporated with unlimited share capital provisions and has no special shares.

You will readily see the information that must be supplied with each application. By using this as a guide and supplying your own information you will be able to complete your own articles.

Given here is a more detailed discussion of the matters to be considered in completing each individual article.

DETAILED INSTRUCTIONS

The numbered headings below correspond to the individual articles as they appear on your Articles of Incorporation form.

1. Name

The name of the corporation should have been submitted to a name search corporation and a report returned to you.

2. Registered office

The registered office, which is where the registers and records of the corporation must be kept must be located in Ontario. The registered office can only be changed by following the procedures set out in section 14 of the Business Corporations Act, 1982.

Give the municipal address of the corporation, including the suite, room or apartment number, where applicable.

If there is no street name or number, use a rural route number. A post office box number may not be used. The example assumes that the business address of the corporation will differ from the residential address of the incorporator or incorporators.

3. Number of directors

As mentioned earlier, you may have one or more directors, or set out a minimum and maximum number. The directors are responsible for conducting the affairs of the corporation. Whether your corporation will have one director, or many, I recommend that you state the number of directors as a minimum of one and a maximum of, say, three, to give you the flexibility for change in the future.

4. First directors

Set out the full names, including first name, initial, and surname, of the directors together with their complete residential addresses, including postal code. A post office box number is not a sufficient residential address. You may change the directors or the number of directors by following the procedure set out in the Business Corporations Act or in the by-laws of your corporation.

A first director who is not an incorporator must consent to act as a first director by filling out Form 2 under the Business Corporations Act, 1982 and such consent must accompany the articles.

See section e of chapter 5, "Shareholders Resolutions."

A majority of the directors must be Canadian citizens and resident in Canada.

5. Restrictions

A corporation incorporated under the Business Corporations Act, 1982, has the capacity and the rights, powers, and privileges of a natural person. Therefore, there is no need to itemize the objects, or the types of business dealings, that the corporation proposes to carry on.

However, you may wish to restrict the corporation by its articles to conducting business within certain bounds. If so, you should set out those restrictions in Article 5. For most corporations, it will not be necessary to do so. If you restrict the type of business that the corporation proposes to carry on, it is important to note that any conduct by the corporation outside of the restrictions in the articles is not necesarily invalid.

6. Class of shares

The Business Corporations Act, 1982, does not provide for an "authorized capital" structure to be set out in the articles as was the case in the past. It requires the articles to include the classes and any maximum number of shares that a corporation is authorized to issue, and if there is more than one class of shares, the conditions for each class.

SAMPLE #10
ARTICLES OF INCORPORATION

For Ministry Use Only
À l'usage exclusif du ministère

Ontario Corporation Number
Numéro de la compagnie en Ontario

Trans Code	Line No.	Stat	Comp Type	Method Incorp.
A	0	0	A	3
18	20	28	29	30

Share	Notice Req'd	Jurisdiction
S	N	ONTARIO
31	32	33 47

ARTICLES OF INCORPORATION
STATUTS CONSTITUTIFS

Form 1
Business
Corporations
Act,
1982

*Formule
numéro 1
Loi de 1982
sur les
compagnies*

1. The name of the corporation is: *Dénomination sociale de la compagnie:*

    J O H N   D O E   A N D   A S S O C I A T E S   L T D

2. The address of the registered office is: *Adresse du siège social:*

    Suite 5600, 390 Bay Street

    (Street & Number or R.R. Number & if Multi-Office Building give Room No.)
    (Rue et numéro ou numéro de la R.R. et, s'il s'agit d'un édifice à bureaux, numéro du bureau)

    Toronto   Z1P 0G0

    (Name of Municipality or Post Office)   (Postal Code)
    (Nom de la municipalité ou du bureau de poste)   *(Code postal)*

    City of Toronto   Municipality of Metropolitan Toronto
                             in the
    (Name of Municipality, Geographical Township)   *dans le/la*   (County, District, Regional Municipality)
    (Nom de la municipalité, du canton)   *(Comté, district, municipalité régionale)*

3. Number (or minimum and maximum number) of   *Nombre (ou nombres minimal et maximal)*
    directors is: *d'administrateurs:*

    A minimum of one and a maximum of three

4. The first director(s) is/are: *Premier(s) administrateur(s):*

First name, initials and surname *Prénom, initiales et nom de famille*	Residence address, giving street & No. or R.R. No. or municipality and postal code. *Adresse personnelle, y compris la rue et le numéro, le numéro de la R.R. ou, le nom de la municipalité et le code postal*	Resident Canadian State Yes or No *Résident Canadien Oui/Non*
John A. Doe	Apt 104, 415 Eglinton Avenue Toronto, Ontario Z1P 0G0	Yes

5. Restrictions, if any, on business the corporation may carry on or on powers the corporation may exercise.

Limites, s'il y a lieu, imposées aux activités commerciales ou aux pouvoirs de la compagnie.

2

NONE

6. The classes and any maximum number of shares that the corporation is authorized to issue.

Catégories et nombre maximal, s'il y a lieu, d'actions que la compagnie est autorisée a émettre:

The Corporation is authorized to issue an unlimited number of common shares.

SAMPLE #10
PAGE 3

3

7. Rights, privileges, restrictions and conditions (if any) attaching to each class of shares and directors authority with respect to any class of shares which may be issued in series:

Droits, privilèges, restrictions et conditions, s'il y a lieu, rattachés à chaque catégorie d'actions et pouvoirs des administrateurs relatifs à chaque catégorie d'actions qui peut être émise en série:

NOT APPLICABLE

SAMPLE #10
PAGE 4

4

8. The issue, transfer or ownership of shares is/~~is not~~ restricted and the restrictions (if any) are as follows:

L'émission, le transfert ou la propriété d'actions est/n'est pas restreinte. Les restrictions, s'il y a lieu, sont les suivantes:

No share of the Corporation shall be transferred without:

either the express consent of the Board of Directors evidenced by a resolution passed at a meeting of directors by the affirmative vote of not less than a majority of the directors or by instrument or instruments in writing signed by   all   of the directors;

or the express consent of the shareholders of the corporation expressed by a resolution passed at a meeting of the holders of such shares or by an instrument or instruments in writing signed by the holders   of all   of the shares.

SAMPLE #10
PAGE 5

5

9. Other provisions, if any, are: *Autres dispositions, s'il y a lieu:*

(1) That the number of shareholders of the Corporation, exclusive of persons who are in its employment and exclusive of persons, who, having been formerly in the employment of the Corporation, were, while in that employment, and have continued after the termination of that employment to be shareholders of the Corporation, is limited to not more than fifty, two or more persons who are the joint registered owners of one or more shares being counted as one shareholder.

(2) That any invitation to the public to subscribe for securities of the Corporation is prohibited.

10. The names and addresses of the incorporators are: *Nom et adresse des fondateurs:*   6

First name, initials and surname or corporate name *Prénom, initiale et nom de famille ou dénomination sociale*	Full residence address or addess of registered office or of principal place of business giving street & No. or R.R. No., municipality and postal code *Adresse personnelle au complet, adresse du siège social ou adresse de l'établissement principal, y compris la rue et le numéro, le numéro de la R.R., le nom de la municipalité et le code postal*
JOHN A. DOE	Apt. 104 415 Eglinton Avenue Toronto, Ontario Z1P 0G0

These articles are signed in duplicate   *Les présents statuts sont signés en double exemplaire.*

Signatures of incorporators
(Signature des fondateurs)

John A. Doe
JOHN A. DOE

If no maximum number of shares is specified, the corporation will have an unlimited number of each class of shares provided for in the articles. As has been the case for some time now, a single incorporation fee is payable regardless of the number of authorized shares.

7. Rights, privileges, restrictions and conditions on each class of share

The Business Corporations Act, 1982, does not prescribe any specific nomenclature for shares. There is no longer a class of common shares to which no conditions are attached; nor is there reference to special or "preference" shares. You only need be concerned with the concept of "shares." Where the corporation has only one class of shares, the rights of all shareholders must be equal in all ways and include the right to vote at all meetings of shareholders and to receive the remaining property of the corporation upon dissolution.

If the articles provide for more than one class of shares, the rights in each class must be stated in the articles. The right to vote and to receive the remaining property upon dissolution must be attached to at least one class of shares, although both rights need not be attached to the same class.

8. Restrictions, transfer, and ownership of shares

The restrictions and special provisions relating to the allotment, issue or transfer of shares as set out in the articles are common for a corporation that is not offering its shares to the public.

The effect of the restrictions is to preserve the status of the corporation as one which does not offer its shares to the public and provides the directors with a measure of control over the transfer of shares.

You may also wish to restrict the ownership of any class of shares to enable the corporation to achieve the status of a Canadian corporation for certain legislative purposes, and accordingly may set out this restriction on ownership in Article 8.

As mentioned, you may choose one of the clauses listed or draft your own.

9. Special provisions

The two special provisions included in the articles are to ensure that the corporation falls within the definition of the term "private company" as set out in the Ontario Securities Act and is, therefore, able to issue its shares without filing a prospectus.

10. Names of incorporators

List the full names and residences of the incorporators. As the form states, full names and address must be provided.

The articles form must also be signed by all of the incorporators.

e. CONSENT TO ACT AS A DIRECTOR

If a person is named as a director who has not signed as an incorporator, his or her consent to act as director must accompany the articles.

The consent form is included with the package kit available from the publisher.

See Sample #11 for an example of a Consent to Act as First Director.

f. CONSENT TO USE OF NAME OF INDIVIDUAL

If the name of the corporation is the same as or includes that of an individual, he or she should file a consent to the use of his or her name together with a statement that he or she has or will have a financial interest in the corporation. (See Sample #12).

This form is also included in the package of forms sold by the publisher.

g. CONSENT TO USE OF NAME OF PARTNERSHIP OR PROPRIETORSHIP

If the corporation is taking over an existing proprietorship or partnership having a name similar to the name proposed for the corporation, a consent signed by the sole proprietor or all partners in the partnership, as the case may be, should be filed with the application, together with an undertaking by the proprietor or partnership to the effect that within six months he or she or they will discontinue business or change the name to a dissimilar one.

A statutory declaration by the sole proprietor or one of the partners, as the case may be, to the effect that he or she is the sole proprietor or that the consent and undertaking to discontinue doing business under that name have been signed by all partners, must accompany the application.

This form is also included in the package kit available from the publisher.

An example of a consent and undertaking form is shown in Sample #13.

h. CONSENT TO USE OF NAME SIMILAR TO EXISTING CORPORATION

If a corporation is assuming a name which is the same as or similar to an existing corporation, a consent signed by the officers of that corporation should be filed with the articles together with an undertaking by that corporation that it will dissolve within six months or change its name to one that is dissimilar.

A consent form is shown in Sample #14. It is the same form as used for a partnership.

i. FILING THE APPLICATION

When the Articles of Incorporation are complete, they should be mailed or delivered to the Companies Branch at 393 University Avenue, Toronto, together with the incorporation fee which is $250.

A covering letter (see Sample #15) should also be sent.

All cheques sent to the Companies Branch must be made payable to the "Treasurer of Ontario" and should be certified. Make sure that you write the name of the corporation on the front of your cheque. If the documents submitted are in order, the Companies Division will stamp your Articles and return them to you. (See Sample #16.)

Form 2
Business
Corporations
Act.
1982
*Formule
numéro 2
Loi de 1982
sur les
compagnies*

CONSENT TO ACT AS A FIRST DIRECTOR
ACCEPTATION DU PREMIER ADMINISTRATEUR

I,/je soussigné(e), _____ Frederick Evan Folio _____

(First name, initials and surname)
(Prénom, initiales et nom de famille)

residing at/*du* _____ Suite 15, 28 Main Street, Toronto, Ontario Z1P 0G0 _____

(Street & No. R.R. No., Municipality & Postal Code)
(Rue et numéro, numéro de la R.R., nom de la municipalité et code postal)

hereby consent to act as a first director of   *accepte par la présente de devenir premier administrateur de*

_____ John Doe and Associates Ltd. _____

(Name of Corporation)
(Dénomination sociale de la compagnie)

_____ *Frederick Evan Folio* _____
Signature of the Consenting Person
Signature de l'acceptant

SAMPLE #12
CONSENT TO USE OF NAME OF INDIVIDUAL

The Business Corporations Act, 1982

CONSENT BY INDIVIDUAL

TO: Companies Services Branch
      Ministry of Consumer and Commercial Relations
      393 University Avenue
      Toronto, Ontario
      M7A 2H6

1.   _John Doe_
     (name of consenting individual; or name of personal representative "on behalf of (insert name of individual")

     Apt. 204, 415 Eglinton Avenue
     (residence address, giving street, number,

     Toronto, Ontario Z1P 0G0
     municipality and postal code)

HEREBY CONSENTS TO THE FOLLOWING NAME FOR USE BY A CORPORATION:

     John Doe and Associates Ltd.
     (proposed name of corporation)

2. THE INDIVIDUAL ABOVE NAMED HAS, HAD, OR WILL HAVE A MATERIAL INTEREST IN THE CORPORATION.

DATED: ___7th January 198-___
       (day, month, year)

                                        John Doe
                                        signature of individual or personal representative

                                        on behalf of _____
                                                     (insert name of individual)

SAMPLE #13
CONSENT OF PARTNERSHIP TO USE OF NAME

The Business Corporations Act, 1982

CONSENT AND UNDERTAKING BY BODY CORPORATE,
PARTNERSHIP, TRUST, ASSOCIATION, ETC.

TO: Companies Services Branch
     Ministry of Consumer and Commercial Relations
     393 University Avenue
     Toronto, Ontario
     M7A 2H6

1.   **JOHN DOE & ASSOCIATES**
    (name of consenting body corporate, partnership, trust, association, etc.)

    222 Eel Avenue,
    (address giving street, number and

    Toronto, Ontario Z1P 0G0
    municipality including postal code)

HEREBY CONSENTS TO THE FOLLOWING NAME FOR USE BY A CORPORATION:

    JOHN DOE & ASSOCIATES LIMITED

    (proposed name of corporation)

2. *   **JOHN DOE & ASSOCIATES**
    (name of consenting body corporate, partnership, trust, association, etc.)

FURTHER UNDERTAKES TO DISSOLVE FORTHWITH OR TO CHANGE ITS NAME TO
SOME DISSIMILAR NAME BEFORE THE SAID CORPORATION PROPOSING TO USE THE
NAME COMMENCES TO USE IT.

DATED: **7th January 198-**
         (day, month, year)

                  John Doe & Associates

                  (name of body corporate, partnership, trust,
                  association, etc.)

(AFFIX CORPORATE SEAL   BY: *John Doe*
HERE IF A CORPORATION)   (signature of authorized official)

                  Partner/president
                  (title of the authorized official)

*strike out if does not apply

40

CORPORATE CONSENT AND UNDERTAKING

FORM 17
The Business Corporations Act, 1982

CONSENT AND UNDERTAKING BY BODY CORPORATE,
PARTNERSHIP, TRUST, ASSOCIATION, ETC.

TO: Companies Services Branch
    Ministry of Consumer and Commercial Relations
    393 University Avenue
    Toronto, Ontario
    M7A 2H6

1.   JOHN DOE & ASSOCIATES INC.
    (name of consenting body corporate, partnership, trust, association, etc.)

    111 Seal Street
    (address giving street, number and

    Toronto, Ontario Z1P 0G0
    municipality including postal code)

HEREBY CONSENTS TO THE FOLLOWING NAME FOR USE BY A CORPORATION:

    JOHN DOE & ASSOCIATES LIMITED
    (proposed name of corporation)

2.   *   JOHN DOE & ASSOCIATES INC.
    (name of consenting body corporate, partnership, trust, association, etc.)

FURTHER UNDERTAKES TO DISSOLVE FORTHWITH OR TO CHANGE ITS NAME TO
SOME DISSIMILAR NAME BEFORE THE SAID CORPORATION PROPOSING TO USE THE
NAME COMMENCES TO USE IT.

DATED: 7   January   198-
        (day, month, year)

                          John Doe & Associates Inc.
                          (name of body corporate, partnership, trust,
                          association, etc.)

(AFFIX CORPORATE SEAL   BY: *John Doe*
HERE IF A CORPORATION)   (signature of authorized official)

                            President
                            (title of the authorized official)

*strike out if does not apply

Ministry of Consumer and Commercial Relations
Companies Branch
393 University Avenue
Toronto, Ontario M7A 2H6

Dear Minister:

Re: Incorporation of John Doe & Associates Limited

Enclosed please find:

1. Executed Articles of Incorporation in duplicate for the above-named proposed corporation with the necessary consent forms (if applicable).

2. Name search forms.

3. Certified cheque in the amount of $250 payable to the Treasurer of Ontario.

Kindly attend to the incorporation of the above-mentioned corporation and return Certificate of Incorporation.

Yours very truly,

John A Doe
_____
John A. Doe

STAMPED ARTICLES OF INCORPORATION

Ministry Use Only
À l'usage exclusif du ministère

Ministry of Consumer and Commercial Relations
Ontario

Ministère de la Consommation et du Commerce

CERTIFICATE
This is to certify that these articles are effective on

CERTIFICAT
Ceci certifie que les présents statuts entrent en vigueur le

SEPTEMBER 30 SEPTEMBRE, 198-

Controller of Records — Contrôleur des Dossiers
Directeur des Compagnies

Ontario Corporation Number
Numéro de la compagnie en Ontario

Trans Code	Line No	Stat	Comp Type	Method Incorp.
A (18)	0 (20)	0 (28)	A (29)	3 (30)

Share	Notice Req'd	Jurisdiction
S (31)	N (32)	ONTARIO (33–47)

ARTICLES OF INCORPORATION
STATUTS CONSTITUTIFS

Form 1
Business Corporations Act, 1982
Formule numéro 1 Loi de 1982 sur les compagnies

1. The name of the corporation is: / *Dénomination sociale de la compagnie:*

JOHN DOE AND ASSOCIATES LTD

2. The address of the registered office is: / *Adresse du siège social:*

Suite 5600, 390 Bay Street
(Street & Number or R.R. Number & if Multi-Office Building give Room No.)
(Rue et numéro ou numéro de la R.R. et, s'il s'agit d'un édifice à bureaux, numéro du bureau)

Toronto
(Name of Municipality or Post Office)
(Nom de la municipalité ou du bureau de poste)

Z1P 0G0 (Postal Code / *Code postal*)

City of Toronto
(Name of Municipality, Geographical Township)
(Nom de la municipalité, du canton)

in the / *dans le/la* Municipality of Metropolitan Toronto
(County, District, Regional Municipality)
(Comté, district, municipalité régionale)

3. Number (or minimum and maximum number) of directors is: / *Nombre (ou nombres minimal et maximal) d'administrateurs:*

A minimum of one and a maximum of three

4. The first director(s) is/are: / *Premier(s) administrateur(s):*

First name, initials and surname / *Prénom, initiales et nom de famille*	Residence address, giving street & No. or R.R. No. or municipality and postal code. / *Adresse personnelle...*	Resident Canadian State Yes or No / *Résident Canadien Oui/Non*
John A. Doe	Apt 104, 415 Eglinton Avenue Toronto, Ontario Z1P 0G0	Yes

43

4

COMPLYING WITH GOVERNMENT REGULATIONS

a. WHAT OTHER LICENCES AND PERMITS DO I NEED?

There are certain government licences and regulations that will affect you and your business. Listed below is a summary of the things you need to know to keep your business and yourself in good standing with the various governments.

Books and records of your company may be audited by federal and provincial agencies from time to time. Therefore, you might as well establish an orderly records and accounts system which will be readily accessible from the beginning.

To do this you will need the help of a good accountant who is familiar with small businesses.

The best way to find someone is to ask your successful business friends, people you admire in a business sense, to supply you with names. Then talk to at least three of them before making a choice.

If you want to learn something about accounting before you talk to an accountant so you can ask some intelligent questions, please refer to *Basic Accounting for the Small Business*, another title in the Self-Counsel Series, for a simplified explanation of the accounting process.

You can expect to have your books examined by the following government departments: Workers' Compensation Board, Revenue Canada — Taxation (which will include payroll auditing of unemployment insurance premiums, Canada Pension Plan contributions, income tax deductions at source), and Revenue Canada — Customs and Excise (for federal sales tax).

The Ontario Corporations Tax Branch will be concerned with your corporation taxes at the provincial level.

You must keep your books and records, including supporting documents — such as sales and purchase invoices, contracts, bank statements, and cancelled cheques — in an orderly manner at your place of business or designated records office.

Revenue Canada — Taxation requires that you keep all business records and supporting documents until you request and obtain written permission from the department to dispose of them. If you wish to destroy company books or records, you must apply in writing to the director of the district taxation office in your area.

You must also provide detailed information identifying the material and the fiscal period covered by such books.

Note: Some records must be kept indefinitely. These include the minute book, share records, general and private ledger sheets, special contracts and agreements, and the general journal if it is essential to the understanding of the general ledger entries.

Other books must be kept until a tax audit or payroll audit has been completed or until at least four years after the taxation year covered, and at that time permission to destroy the records may be given.

b. FEDERAL REQUIREMENTS AND REGULATIONS YOU SHOULD KNOW ABOUT

1. Federal sales tax

The federal government levies a sales tax, with certain exceptions, on the sale price of goods manufactured or produced in Canada. The manufacturer or producer is required to pay this at the time of delivery to the purchaser.

This federal sales tax is also applied, with some exceptions, to the customs duty-paid value of goods imported for consumption in Canada.

Items exempt from sales tax include practically all foodstuffs, goods consumed in a manufacturing process, machinery and apparatus used in the manufacture and production of goods and implements utilized in the agriculture and fishing industries.

Tax refunds are available on construction materials used to construct educational institutions and libraries.

If you are a manufacturer, you must obtain a sales tax licence which is issued by the federal Sales and Excise Tax Office, Revenue Canada, and permits you to purchase or import articles and materials free of sales tax when certified to be used in, wrought into, or attached to taxable goods for resale.

There are instances in which this tax is applied at the wholesale level.

Information on all sales taxes, including the procedure for filing returns and paying taxes, can be obtained from the federal Sales and Excise Tax Office, Revenue Canada — Customs and Excise.

2. Federal excise tax

An excise tax, in addition to the sales tax, is imposed on certain specific goods, whether manufactured or produced in Canada or imported into Canada.

The list of excisable items includes — among others — jewellery, matches, cigarettes, and tobacco.

Complete details can be found in the Excise Tax Act, a copy of which may be ordered from the Canadian Government Publications Centre, Supply and Services Canada, Hull, Quebec, K1A 0S9. Some bookstores also carry copies of the act.

Revenue Canada — Customs and Excise requires that all persons or firms manufacturing or producing goods subject to an excise tax must operate under a manufacturer's excise tax licence.

The licence is obtainable from the regional or district Excise Tax Office, Revenue Canada, in the area in which you or your company proposes to operate.

Manufacturers licensed for excise tax purposes may purchase or import, free from excise tax, goods that are to be incorporated into and form a constituent or component part of an article or product that is subject to an excise tax, provided they quote their excise tax licence number and relevant certificate.

The procedure for filing returns and paying excise tax is similar to that for sales tax. If you are in any doubt concerning your status under the Excise Tax Act, write to the Regional Director, Revenue Canada — Customs and Excise.

3. Customs duties

Any business that imports products from abroad must be aware of customs duties, which are levied against goods upon entry into Canada.

There are regulations concerning invoicing, classification of goods, rates of duty and reductions and exemptions for special classes of articles. It is advisable for you to obtain a ruling on the classification, rate of duty, and valuation prior to commencing shipments.

Foreign exporters and Canadian importers are advised to approach the regional collector of customs, Revenue Canada, having jurisdiction over the Canadian port of entry for the majority of their goods.

4. Federal income tax

The federal government levies both personal and corporate income tax on monies earned in Canada. Income taxes are applied on income received or receivable during the taxation year from all sources inside and outside Canada, less certain deductions.

Individuals and branches of foreign companies carrying on business in Canada are also liable for income taxes on profits derived from these business operations. Small businesses qualify for special tax rates (see chapter 2 on tax advantages for further information).

If you are an employer, you are required to deduct personal income tax from the pay cheques of all employees on a regular basis. Remit these funds monthly through any branch of a chartered bank or to the Taxation Data Centre, Ottawa, Ontario.

Deduction of employee benefits must be made from the date of commencement of work. The federal income tax regulations outline the rules for allocating income to provinces when individuals earn business income in more than one province.

For specific information about federal income tax, contact the nearest office of Revenue Canada — Taxation.

5. Unemployment insurance

In Canada, workers who become unemployed may qualify for unemployment insurance benefits under a federal government program. The program is administered by the Unemployment Insurance Commission.

With few exceptions, all employment in Canada performed under a contract of service is insurable, and, therefore, subject to unemployment insurance premium payments by both the employer and the employee.

The employer is required to collect employee's premiums in accordance with the current premium scales. All matters relating to deductions, remittances, and ruling for unemployment insurance premiums are handled by Revenue Canada — Taxation.

6. Canada Pension Plan

The Canada Pension Plan is designed to provide a basic retirement pension for working Canadians. Employees between the ages of 18 and 70 in most types of employment are covered by the plan and must contribute.

Types of non-pensionable employment include agriculture, horticulture, fishing, hunting, forestry, logging or lumbering where the employee earns less than $250 in cash per year.

The employer is responsible for making the deductions from all eligible employees and must match these deductions with similar contributions. A person who is self-employed is responsible for the entire annual contribution to the Canada Pension Plan.

Note: If you are incorporated and pay yourself a wage, as far as the Canada Pension Plan is concerned you are not self-employed. You should deduct the normal amount from your wage and the company will also contribute as the employer.

Revenue Canada — Taxation can help employers calculate the amount of unemployment insurance, Canada Pension Plan and income tax deductions to be made from employees' salaries. When you apply for an account number, they will supply you with the charts to calculate the deductions, along with an explanatory book.

The employer must remit these funds through any branch of a chartered bank or the Taxation Data Centre, Ottawa, Ontario.

c. PROVINCIAL GOVERNMENT REQUIREMENTS AND REGULATIONS YOU SHOULD KNOW ABOUT

1. Licensing

There are certain specific provincial acts containing licensing regulations and requirements which apply to specific businesses.

While it is impossible to list all the provincial acts and the businesses to which they apply, the following is a list of areas which fall under provincial jurisdiction and about which you should be concerned if you operate a business in these areas.

(a) Door-to-door sales, pyramid schemes, franchises
(b) Firms that loan money or are involved in any way with the consumer finance business
(c) Manufacturers (especially regarding labor laws and factory standards)

(d) Anyone who handles or processes food

(e) Anyone who is in the transport (goods or persons) business

(f) Anyone who is dealing with the natural resources, such as forests, minerals, or water

(g) Anyone in the fish processing business

(h) Anyone who is affected by pollution standards

(i) Anyone who does business on provincially-owned land, such as parks and beaches

2. Sales tax

Every provincial government, with the exception of the one in Alberta, imposes a "social service" tax. At present in Ontario the sales tax is 8%, which is levied on virtually all tangible personal property that is purchased or imported for consumption or use. This tax is collected from the ultimate consumer who resides in Ontario by the seller.

If you are going to be buying merchandise for resale, you will need to apply for a provincial tax number. Upon application, a registration certificate assigning a tax number will be issued by the Ontario retail sales tax branch.

This certificate grants exemption from the payment of the tax on merchandise which is purchased for resale purposes or for merchandise which will become part of tangible personal property intended for resale.

3. Power to hold land

In the past, Ontario had laws known as mortmain laws which made it necessary for a corporation to obtain a licence in order to hold land. However, this was repealed in 1982.

It is important to note, however, that a corporation incorporated in a jurisdiction other than Canada that obtains an extra-provincial licence in Ontario, has the capacity to acquire, purchase, and hold land. This procedure is outlined in chapter 12.

4. The Workers' Compensation Board

Ontario was one of the first provinces in Canada to establish a means by which all employers insured themselves against claims by injured workers. The board provides compensation to injured employees from a fund paid into by all employers. The size of each employer's payment depends upon the nature of the industry that most of the workers are engaged in and the amount of the payroll.

If your proprietorship or partnership already has employees, the Workers' Compensation Board will be no stranger to you. However, for those of you who have operated as a proprietorship or partner with no employees you should know that upon incorporating a one-person corporation, you become an "executive officer" who is exempt by choice *and* an employee. In this event, you should contact the board to find out whether or not the Workers' Compensation Act applies to your particular industry and situation. If your corporation pays you salary or wages, or makes payments pursuant to a contract of employment, you may be classed as an employee and your corporation regarded as an employer.

However, employers, partners, and their spouses who work for the partnership, independent operators, and directors or executive officers or professional corporations can, in many cases, elect whether or not they wish to be covered by the act. If they choose to be covered they must either estimate their earnings at a rate which is reasonable to the board or, in the case of executive officers of corporations, their earnings, subject to the maximum allowed by the act, are the basis for accident fund assessments.

If you employ sub-contractors or independent operators to do work for you and they are not covered by the board, you will be responsible for furnishing a payroll statement for the employees of the contractor. The statement will show the money paid into the board on behalf of the contractor's employees.

The fees and assessments are to be borne entirely by the employers; no deductions may be made from the employees's wages to cover assessments.

If you are planning to incorporate and then engage in a business like logging, mining, manufacturing, or even farming, you should contact the board prior to incorporation to find out what their procedures are and, in cases of "high risk" businesses, take out coverage so that employees of the corporation are covered from day one and you will not be liable for an accident.

Certainly if you are not prepared for Workers' Compensation Board assessments and filings, they can cause you a lot of grief. For this reason I suggest that you inquire at your local office immediately after, or before, incorporating. It is highly likely that you will be responsible for some sort of assessment if you operate as a one-person corporation, where you may not have been liable previously when you did business as a sole proprietor.

Following is a list of Workers' Compensation Board Offices:

Toronto

Head office:
2 Bloor Street East,
Toronto M4W 3C3
(416) 927-9555
Metro Toronto Information Centre
1382 St. Clair Avenue West
Toronto M6E 1C6
(416) 965-8864

Hamilton

Plaza level
Standard Life Centre
2 King Street West
Hamilton L8P 1A1
(416) 523-1800

Kingston

1055 Princess Street
Room 303
Kingston K7L 5T3
(613) 544-9682

Kitchener-Waterloo

153 Frederick Street,
Kitchener N2H 2M1
(519) 576-4130

London

200 Queens Avenue, Second Floor
London N6A 1J3
(519) 663-2331

North Bay

189 Wyld Street,
North Bay P1B 1Z2
(705) 472-5200

Ottawa

350 Sparks Street, Room 206
Ottawa K1R 7S8
(613) 238-7851

Sault Ste. Marie

3rd Floor,
421 Bay Street,
Sault Ste. Marie P6A 1X3
(705) 942-3002

St. Catharines

161 Carlton Street
Suite 201
St. Catharines L2R 1R5
(416) 687-8622

Sudbury

30 Cedar Street, Fifth Floor
Subury P3E 1A4
(705) 675-9301

Thunder Bay

420 Memorial Avenue
Thunder Bay P7C 5S2
(807) 343-1710

Timmins
273 Third Avenue, Suite 204
Timmins P4N 1E2
(705) 267-6427

Windsor
787 Ouellette Avenue,
Windsor N9A 4J4
(519) 256-3461

Registrar of Appeals
The Workers' Compensation Board
2 Bloor Street East,
Toronto M4W 3C3
(416) 965-8926

d. MUNICIPAL GOVERNMENT REQUIREMENTS AND REGULATIONS YOU SHOULD KNOW ABOUT

1. Licensing

The Municipal Act authorizes municipalities to license all businesses within its boundaries. Incorporated centres issue licences and permits based on local by-laws.

Communities can control aspects of zoning, land use, construction and renovation for all types of business activities including the licensing of commercial vehicles.

Contact the local city hall or municipal office for information in these areas. In unincorporated areas, contact the nearest government agent or RCMP detachment.

2. Municipal taxes

Municipal governments levy direct taxes on real estate, water consumption, and business premises.

Property taxes are based on the assessed real value of land and improvements. Annual notices of assessments are sent out with provision for appeal.

Local business taxes are applied directly against the tenant or the business operator. The business tax is generally based on a percentage of the annual rental value, the property assessment or the size of the premises.

3. Building requirements

All three levels of government have some responsibility for regulating commercial building. Any construction which is proposed must satisfy all the requirements of the three governments.

The city hall or municipal office brings together all the various building codes and inspections making it possible for approval of planned construction to be obtained at the local level.

The municipality controls the type of building you may construct. Municipal building and zoning regulations control the physical structure and the final use of your building. The municipality also has the power to enforce building regulations.

Before beginning construction or renovation of a structure, you must obtain a building permit from the municipality. To apply, you must submit preliminary sketches for approval and, when the sketches have received approval, submit complete construction drawings which will be examined to ensure that they meet the federal, provincial and municipal building standards. If approval is given, then you will be issued a building permit.

Once construction has commenced, various stages of the construction must be inspected before the project can continue.

As each municipality controls certain aspects of construction, the requirements vary from one area to another so you should contact the building department of the municipal government office for specific requirements.

e. MISCELLANEOUS INFORMATION YOU SHOULD KNOW ABOUT

1. The metric system

The metric system is simple to use because relationships are in powers of ten. Approximately 90% of the world's population is using or converting to the metric system.

It is important that you be aware of what you need to do to comply with the system.

For information on how metric conversion may affect your business, contact the provincial Department of Economic Development or write to —

Measurement Information Division
Consumer and Corporate Affairs
P.O. Box 4000
Ottawa, Ontario
K1A 5G8

2. Weights and measures

The Department of Consumer and Corporate Affairs is responsible for the approval and initial inspection of all weighing and measuring devices, such as scales and fuel dispensers that are used in trade.

The Weights and Measures Branch must inspect all new trade devices prior to first use. If you acquire used weighing equipment for commercial use, you should notify the Weights and Measures Branch.

Those devices requiring installation before being inspected, (e.g., vehicle scales), must be inspected on site when operational. Movable devices may be factory inspected prior to shipping and the department must be notified when this equipment is in place.

Any relocation of the equipment must be reported to the department to ensure that regular inspections can continue to take place.

The period between inspections varies but is usually every two years. You should note that you are responsible for the cost of the initial inspections.

For further information or to arrange for an inspection, contact the nearest Weights and Measures office of the federal department of Consumer and Corporate Affairs.

3. Packaging and labelling

Any prepackaged consumer product, including food and non-food items, is subject to the packaging regulations of the federal Department of Consumer and Corporate Affairs.

Prepackaged products require a label that states the product's net quantity. The information must be declared in metric units, and optionally in Canadian units of measure and must appear in French and English. The identity of the product must also be given in both French and English.

The identity and principal place of business of the manufacturer or the person for whom the product was manufactured must appear on the package in either French or English.

In some instances other information may be required. For example, hazardous or dangerous products must be properly marked, according to the Hazardous Products Act.

Textiles must be labelled with the fibre content according to the Textile Labelling Act. This act provides for the mandatory labelling of such textile articles as wearing apparel, fabrics sold by the piece, and household textiles. It also regulates the advertising, sale, and importation of all consumer textile fabric products.

Articles such as jewellery, silverware, optical products, watches, pens, and pencils, which are made wholly or partly of precious metals, are regulated by the Precious Metals Marketing Act.

There are restrictions on the permissible size of the packages and for certain products only specific sizes are allowed. The federal Department of Consumer and Corporate Affairs should be contacted for detailed information regarding packaging.

4. Patents, copyright, trade marks, and industrial designs

The laws concerning patents, copyright, trade marks, and industrial designs are very complicated and you may find professional help useful. Patent and trade marks lawyers specialize in these fields and can ensure that you get the maximum protection and benefit. Look in the yellow pages or phone your local lawyer referral service to find the patent and trade marks agents available to you. Before you see a lawyer you might find it helpful to call or write to your nearest federal Consumer and Corporate Affairs office. They have free pamphlets concerning trade marks, patents, copyright and industrial design. These pamphlets will provide a useful introduction to the subject and familiarize you with the terms used.

For patents, if you have not yet completed your invention and are concerned that others might patent it, you may file in the patent office a description of the invention insofar as it has been developed.

The document filed is known as a "caveat." You, the "caveator," will be informed if anyone else files an application to patent the same invention in the year immediately following the filing of the caveat.

The caveat may also have some value in proving when your invention was made. It does not give you any right to exclude others from using the invention. It is not until you have filed an application for patent and been granted a patent that you are entitled to any exclusive rights to the invention. A caveat is not an application for patent, and its value is limited.

The various offices of the Department of Consumer and Corporate Affairs throughout the region can provide information regarding patents, copyrights, trade marks, and industrial designs and can also accept for dating and transmission to Ottawa applications for these various forms of protection of intellectual property.

(a) Patents

A patent is a contract between the federal government and an inventor. In exchange for full disclosure of the invention, the government will grant the inventor the exclusive right to make, use, or sell the invention in Canada for 17 years.

Patents are granted for inventions defined as some technological development or improvement that has not previously been considered.

If you wish to apply for a patent, you must make an application to the Commissioner of Patents, Ottawa, Canada. The application must meet all the requirements of the Patent Act and the Patent Rules. For more information, see *Patent Your Own Invention in Canada*, another title in the Self-Counsel Series.

(b) Copyright

Under the Canadian Copyright Act, copyright subsists automatically in every original literary, musical, dramatic, and artistic work when in a *permanent* form; registration is merely proof of ownership. The author must be a Canadian national, a British subject, or a citizen of a country which adheres to the Universal Copyright Convention when he or she produced the work.

The author's rights are recognized as existing once he or she has produced the work. This exclusive right lasts for the life of the author and 50 years after the author's death.

In the case of records, discs, and photographs, the term of protection is 50 years, irrespective of the lifespan of the author.

To register a copyright, you must send your application to the Registrar of Copyright in Ottawa on the form prescribed in the Copyright Rules. The cost is $35.

Copies of the Copyright Act and Rules can be ordered from the Canadian Government Publications Centre, Hull, Quebec, K1A 0S9.

(c) Trade marks

The Trade Marks Act governs trade mark registration in Canada and provides for the registration of trade marks used in association with services or wares.

Registration, although advisable, is not compulsory; however, a registered mark is more easily protected than an unregistered trade mark.

Registration of a trade mark endures for 15 years and is renewable. The Trade Marks Act outlines the types of symbols that can or cannot be registered.

When sending an application for registration of a trade mark, you must include the filing fee of $150. After the application has been allowed, a further fee of $200 is required for registration of the mark.

The application may be submitted by you, the owner of the trade mark, or your authorized agent. The application is submitted to the Registrar of Trade Marks, Department of Consumer and Corporate Affairs, Ottawa.

There are no forms for a trade mark application, but the information must be supplied as outlined in the publication *Trade Marks: Questions and Answers*, which is available free from the Canadian Government Publications Centre.

(d) Industrial designs

An industrial design is any original shape, pattern, or ornamentation applied to an article of manufacture. The industrial design must be made by an industrial process.

An industrial design may be registered in Canada if the design is not identical or similar to others registered. The design must be registered within one year of publication in this country.

Registration provides you with exclusive right to the design for a period of five years. Registration may be extended for one additional five-year period.

To register a design, you must file a drawing and description with the Registrar of Industrial Design in Ottawa. A search will be made of earlier designs to determine if the design is novel.

Note: Inquiries about copyright, patents, trade marks, and industrial designs should be directed to the Department of Consumer and Corporate Affairs, Ottawa.

5. Immigration and citizenship

If you are established in business in a foreign country but wish to live and establish a business in Canada, you must contact the Canadian immigration representative in your country.

It is necessary to apply for permanent resident status while still outside Canada. If you satisfy the immigration officer about the feasibility of your business proposal and you meet all other immigration requirements, it is possible that you will receive permanent resident status.

Canadian citizenship is usually not needed for employment in Canada except in certain areas of the civil service and some professions. If you are considering employment, other than on a temporary basis, permanent resident status must be applied for prior to your arrival in Canada.

Full citizenship can be applied for after three years' residence in Canada.

The duty-free entry of effects owned by persons prior to coming to Canada is provided by Canadian customs regulations. Such goods may not be sold or otherwise disposed of within 12 months of entry without payment of duty.

If you plan to bring with you tools or machinery necessary for your business or profession, be sure to make arrangements before you have them shipped. Customs duty and sales tax are applicable to equipment and you should be aware of the requirements.

Further information on the above may be obtained from the nearest Canadian embassy or consulate or by writing to the Department of Employment and Immigration, Ottawa.

5

POST-INCORPORATION PROCEDURES

When a Certificate of Incorporation is issued, a new legal entity is created. This means it can sue or be sued or can enter into contracts on its own behalf. The following pages outline the steps to be taken to complete the organization of the corporation and to preserve its status.

a. PURCHASE OF MINUTE BOOK, SEAL, AND SHARE CERTIFICATES

The Business Corporations Act, 1982, subject to certain exceptions which will not be discussed here, requires that certain records of the corporation be kept at its registered office in a bound or looseleaf book or by means of a mechanical, electronic or other device. Most self-incorporators do very well with the bound or looseleaf book as a means of recording and collecting all corporate documents.

Records to be kept include the following:

(a) A copy of the Articles of Incorporation, by-laws, and any unanimous shareholder agreement known to the directors
(b) All resolutions of the corporation
(c) A register of security holders alphabetically indexed in appropriate categories as to shareholders and holders of debt obligations and warrants, together with the particulars of each
(d) A register of directors
(e) Accounting records
(f) A register of share transfers

Minute books that contain all the necessary registers may be purchased from the publisher. If you are making use of the publisher's phone-in typing service, the minutes of the incorporators' and first directors' meetings will be typed up for you.

By adding your Articles of Incorporation, resolutions as passed, and minutes of meetings of directors or shareholders, if held, you can keep your records in one book. You are also required to institute a proper set of financial or accounting records for the corporation.

The package of forms supplied by the publisher includes share certificates. For the purpose of executing most documents in Ontario, you will require a corporate seal. The seal must be endorsed with the exact name of the corporation as set out in its articles and for this reason should not be ordered until the Certificate of Incorporation is received. A seal may also be ordered from the publisher with the order form at the front of the book.

b. ORGANIZING THE CORPORATION

1. By-laws and resolutions

By-laws of the corporation are rules that govern its internal affairs. Resolutions are the acts of the shareholders or directors governing the course of the business of the corporation (e.g., you pass a resolution to appoint a new director).

The act provides for the passage of by-laws and resolutions either at meetings of shareholders or directors, as the case may be, or by written consent of all the shareholders or directors. Your way of conducting the corporation's business will depend upon the situation you are in.

In small closely held corporations, it is usually more convenient to pass resolutions and by-laws by written consent. For this reason, details about the notice periods required for calling meetings and who must be present are not discussed here. The post-incorporation procedures set out here are all based on the passage of resolutions and by-laws by the written consent of all shareholders and directors.

You may have ordinary or special resolutions. An ordinary resolution is one that is submitted to a meeting of the shareholders and passed by at least a majority of the votes cast.

A special resolution is one submitted to a special meeting of the shareholders duly called for the purpose of considering the resolution, and passed by at least two-thirds of the votes cast, or alternatively consented to by each shareholder in writing.

Unless otherwise provided by the articles, the by-laws, or a unanimous shareholder agreement, the directors may, either with a quorum at a meeting, or unanimously in writing by resolution, enact a by-law that regulates the business or affairs of the corporation, and they shall submit the by-law to the shareholders at the next meeting of shareholders for confirmation, or alternatively obtain the written consent of the shareholders.

A general by-law or resolution can be passed and become effective immediately and continues in effect when confirmed by the shareholders. A special resolution must be confirmed by the shareholders before it can become effective.

If a by-law is not confirmed at the annual shareholders' meeting or at a prior meeting of shareholders or in writing by all shareholders entitled to vote, that particular by-law or a similar by-law ceases to be effective on the date it was rejected by the shareholders.

Resolutions are valid on the date they are passed by the directors and shareholders, and continue to be valid until revoked or changed by resolutions of directors that are either immediately or eventually confirmed by shareholders at the annual general meeting.

2. The general by-law

Sample #17 shows a general by-law designed for use by almost any type or size of corporation. This set is included with the package of incorporation forms available from the publisher.

A lawyer should be consulted if you wish to make any substantive amendments to them. The set, as it will be adopted by your corporation, should be read carefully to ensure that you comply with it in carrying on business.

You adopt the general by-law by having all the shareholders and directors place their signature at the end on the last page, and by setting out the date on which all of the shareholders and directors consented to the adoption of the general by-law.

BY-LAW NO. 1

**A by-law relating generally to the
transaction of the business and affairs of**
John Doe and Associates Ltd.
(herein called the "corporation")

CONTENTS

BE IT ENACTED as a by-law of the corporation as follows:

Section One

INTERPRETATION

1.01 **Definitions.** In this by-law, unless the context otherwise requires:

(i) words importing the singular include the plural and vice versa and words importing gender include the masculine, feminine and neuter genders;

(ii) "Act" means the Business Corporations Act, 1982, and includes the regulations made pursuant thereto;

(iii) "board" means the board of directors of the corporation;

(iv) "number of directors" means the number of directors provided for in the articles or, where a minimum and maximum number of directors is provided for in the articles, the number of directors determined by a special resolution or resolution passed pursuant to subsection 125(2) of the Act.

(v)   words and expressions defined in the Act shall have the same meanings when used herein.

Section Two

BUSINESS OF THE CORPORATION

2.01 Financial Year. Until changed by the board, the financial year of the corporation shall end on the last day of   in each year.

2.02 Execution of Instruments. Deeds, transfers, assignments, contracts, obligations, certificates and other instruments may be signed on behalf of the corporation by two persons, one of whom holds the office of chairman of the board, president, managing director, vice–president or director and the other of whom holds one of the said offices or the office of secretary, treasurer, assistant secretary or assistant treasurer or any other office created by by-law or by resolution of the board. In addition, the board may from time to time direct the manner in which the person or persons by whom any particular instrument or class of instruments may or shall be signed.

Section Three

DIRECTORS

3.01 Quorum. The quorum for the transaction of business at any meeting of the board shall consist of a majority of the number of directors.

3.02 Qualification. No person shall be qualified for election as a director if he is less then eighteen years of age; if he is of unsound mind and has been so found by a court in Canada or elsewhere; if he is not an individual; or if he has the status of a bankrupt. A director need not be a shareholder. A majority of the directors shall be resident Canadians provided that if the number of directors is two, at least one shall be a resident Canadian.

3.03 Election and Term. The election of directors shall take place at the first meeting of shareholders and at each annual meeting of shareholders and all the directors then in office shall retire but, if qualified, shall be eligible for re-election. The election shall be by resolution. If an election of directors is not held at the proper time, the incumbent directors shall continue in office until their successors are elected.

3.04 Removal of Directors. Subject to the provisions of the Act, the shareholders may by resolution passed at an annual or special meeting remove any director from office and the vacancy created by such removal may be filled at the same meeting failing which it may be filled by the directors.

3.05 Vacation of Office. A director ceases to hold office when he dies; he is removed from office by the shareholders; he ceases to be qualified for election as a director; or his written resignation is sent or delivered to the corporation, or if a time is specified in such resignation, at the time so specified, whichever is later.

3.06 Vacancies. Subject to the Act, a quorum of the board may fill a vacancy in the board, except a vacancy resulting from an increase in the number of directors or in the maximum number of directors or from a failure of the shareholders to elect the number of directors. In the absence of a quorum of the board, or if the vacancy has arisen from a failure of the shareholders to elect the number of directors, the board shall forthwith call a special meeting of shareholders to fill the vacancy. If the board fails to call such meeting or if there are no such directors then in office, any shareholder may call the meeting.

3.07 Canadian Majority. The board shall not transact business at a meeting, other than filling a vacancy in the board, unless a majority of the directors are resident Canadians, except where

(a) a resident Canadian director who is unable to be present approves in writing or by telephone or other communications facilities the business transacted at the meeting; and

(b) a majority of resident Canadians would have been present had that director been present at the meeting.

3.08 Meetings by Telephone. If all the directors consent, a director may participate in a meeting of the board or of a committee of the board by means of such telephone or other communications facilities as permit all persons participating in the meeting to hear each other, and a director participating in such a meeting by such means is deemed to be present at the meeting. Any such consent shall be effective whether given before or after the meeting to which it relates and may be given with respect to all meetings of the board and of committees of the board held while a director holds office.

3.09 Place of Meetings. Meetings of the board may be held at any place within or without Ontario. In any financial year of the corporation a majority of the meetings of the board need not be held within Canada.

3.10 Calling of Meetings. Meetings of the board shall be held from time to time and at such place as the board, the chairman of the board, the managing director, the president or any two directors may determine.

3.11 Notice of Meeting. Notice of the time and place of each meeting of the board shall be given in the manner provided in section 10.01 to each director not less than forty-eight hours before the time when the meeting is to be held. A notice of a meeting of directors need not specify the purpose of or the

Page 4

business to be transacted at the meeting except where the Act requires such purpose or business to be specified. A director may in any manner waive notice of or otherwise consent to a meeting of the board.

3.12 Adjourned Meeting. Notice of an adjourned meeting of the board is not required if the time and place of the adjourned meeting is announced at the original meeting.

3.13 Regular Meetings. The board may appoint a day or days in any month or months for regular meetings of the board at a place and hour to be named. A copy of any resolution of the board fixing the place and time of such regular meetings shall be sent to each director forthwith after being passed, but no other notice shall be required for any such regular meeting except where the Act requires the purpose thereof or the business to be transacted thereat to be specified.

3.14 Chairman. The chairman of any meeting of the board shall be the first mentioned of such of the following officers as have been appointed and who is a director and is present at the meeting: chairman of the board, managing director, president, or a vice-president who is a director. If no such officer is present, the directors present shall choose one of their number to be chairman.

3.15 Votes to Govern. At all meetings of the board every question shall be decided by a majority of the votes cast on the question. In case of an equality of votes the chairman of the meeting shall be entitled to a second or casting vote.

3.16 Conflict of Interest. A director or officer who is a party to, or who is a director or officer of or has a material interest in any person who is a party to, a material contract or proposed material contract with the corporation shall disclose the nature and extent of his interest at the time and in the manner provided by the Act. Any such contract or proposed contract shall be referred to the board or shareholders for approval even if such contract is one that in the ordinary course of the corporation's business would not require approval by the board or shareholders, and a director interested in a contract so referred to the board shall not vote on any resolution to approve the same except as provided by the Act.

3.17 Remuneration and Expenses. Subject to the articles or any unanimous shareholder agreement, the directors shall be paid such remuneration for their services as the board may from time to time determine. The directors shall also be entitled to be reimbursed for travelling and other expenses properly incurred by them in attending meetings of the board or any committee thereof. Nothing herein contained shall preclude any director from serving the corporation in any other capacity and receiving remuneration therefor.

Page 5

Section Four

COMMITTEES

4.01 Committee of Directors. The board may appoint a committee of directors, however designated, and delegate to such committee any of the powers of the board except those which, under the Act, a committee of directors has no authority to exercise. A majority of the members of such committee shall be resident Canadians.

4.02 Transaction of Business. The powers of a committee of directors may be exercised by a meeting at which a quorum is present or by resolution in writing signed by all the members of such committee who would have been entitled to vote on that resolution at a meeting of the committee. Meetings of such committee may be held at any place within or without Ontario.

4.03 Procedure. Unless otherwise determined by the board, each committee shall have the power to fix its quorum at not less than a majority of its members, to elect its chairman and to regulate its procedure.

Section Five

OFFICERS

5.01 Appointment. Subject to any unanimous shareholder agreement, the board may from time to time appoint a president, one or more vice-presidents (to which title may be added words indicating seniority or function), a secretary, a treasurer and such other officers as the board may determine, including one or more assistants to any of the officers so appointed. The board may specify the duties of and, in accordance with this by-law and subject to the provisions of the Act, delegate to such officers powers to manage the business and affairs of the corporation.

5.02 Chairman of the Board. The board may from time to time also appoint a chairman of the board who shall be a director. If appointed, the board may assign to him any of the powers and duties that are by any provisions of this by-law assigned to the managing director or to the president; and he shall, subject to the provisions of the Act, the articles or any unanimous shareholder agreement, have such other powers and duties as the board may specify. During the absence or disability of the chairman of the board, his duties shall be performed and his powers exercised by the managing director, if any, or by the president.

5.03 Managing Director. The board may from time to time appoint a managing director who shall be a resident Canadian and a director. If appointed, he shall be the chief executive officer and, subject to the authority of the board,

Page 6

shall have general supervision of the business and affairs of the corporation; and he shall, subject to the provisions of the Act or the articles, have such other powers and duties as the board may specify. During the absence or disability of the president, or if no president has been appointed, the managing director shall also have the powers and duties of that office.

5.04 President. If appointed, the president shall be the chief operating officer and, subject to the authority of the board, shall have general supervision of the business of the corporation; and he shall have such other powers and duties as the board may specify. During the absence or disability of the managing director, or if no managing director has been appointed, the president shall also have the powers and duties of that office.

5.05 Vice-President. A vice-president shall have such powers and duties as the board or the chief executive officer may specify.

5.06 Secretary. The secretary shall attend and be the secretary of all meetings of the board, shareholders and committees of the board and shall enter or cause to be entered in records kept for that purpose minutes of all proceedings thereat; he shall give or cause to be given, as and when instructed, all notices to shareholders, directors, officers, auditors and members of committees of the board; he shall be the custodian of all books, papers, records, documents and instruments belonging to the corporation, except when some other officer or agent has been appointed for that purpose; and he shall have such other powers and duties as the board or the chief executive officer may specify.

5.07 Treasurer. The treasurer shall keep proper accounting records in compliance with the Act and shall be responsible for the deposit of money, the safekeeping of securities and the disbursement of the funds of the corporation; he shall render to the board whenever required an account of all his transactions as treasurer and of the financial position of the corporation; and he shall have such other powers and duties as the board or the chief executive officer may specify.

5.08 Powers and Duties of Other Officers. The powers and duties of all other officers shall be such as the terms of their engagement call for or as the board or the chief executive officer may specify. Any of the powers and duties of an officer to whom an assistant has been appointed may be exercised and performed by such assistant, unless the board or the chief executive officer otherwise directs.

5.09 Variation of Powers and Duties. The board may from time to time and subject to the provisions of the Act, vary, add to or limit the powers and duties of any officer.

5.10 Term of Office. The board, in its discretion, may remove any officer of the corporation, without prejudice to such officer's rights under any employment contract. Otherwise each officer appointed by the board shall hold office until his successor is appointed.

Section Six

PROTECTION OF DIRECTORS, OFFICERS AND OTHERS

6.01 Limitation of Liability. No director or officer shall be liable for the acts, receipts, neglects or defaults of any other director or officer or employee, or for joining in any receipt or other act for conformity, or for any loss, damage or expense happening to the corporation through the insufficiency or deficiency of title to any property acquired for or on behalf of the corporation, or for the insufficiency or deficiency of any security in or upon which any of the moneys of the corporation shall be invested, or for any loss or damage arising from the bankruptcy, insolvency or tortious acts of any person with whom any of the moneys, securities or effects of the corporation shall be deposited, or for any loss occasioned by any error of judgment or oversight on his part, or for any other loss, damage or misfortune whatever which shall happen in the execution of the duties of his office or in relation thereto, unless the same are occasioned by his own wilful neglect or default; provided that nothing herein shall relieve any director or officer from the duty to act in accordance with the Act and the regulations thereunder or from liability for any breach thereof.

6.02 Indemnity. Subject to the limitations contained in the Act, the corporation shall indemnify a director or officer, a former director or officer, or a person who acts or acted at the corporation's request as a director or officer of a body corporate of which the corporation is or was a shareholder or creditor (or a person who undertakes or has undertaken any liability on behalf of the corporation or any such body corporate) and his heirs and legal representatives, against all costs, charges and expenses, including an amount paid to settle an action or satisfy a judgment, reasonably incurred by him in respect of any civil, criminal or administrative action or proceeding to which he is made a party by reason of being or having been a director or officer of the corporation or such body corporate, if

(a) he acted honestly and in good faith with a view to the best interests of the corporation; and

(b) in the case of a criminal or administrative action or proceeding that is enforced by a monetary penalty, he had reasonable grounds for believing that his conduct was lawful.

6.03 Insurance. Subject to the limitations contained in the Act, the corporation may purchase and maintain such insurance for the benefit of its directors and officers as such, as the board may from time to time determine.

Page 8

Section Seven

SHARES

7.01 Allotment. The board may from time to time allot or grant options to purchase the whole or any part of the authorized and unissued shares of the corporation at such times and to such persons and for such consideration as the board shall determine, provided that no share shall be issued until it is fully paid as prescribed by the Act.

7.02 Commissions. The board may from time to time authorize the corporation to pay a commission to any person in consideration of his purchasing or agreeing to purchase shares of the corporation, whether from the corporation or from any other person, or procuring or agreeing to procure purchasers for any such shares.

7.03 Registration of Transfer. Subject to the provisions of the Act, no transfer of shares shall be registered in a securities register except upon presentation of the certificate representing such shares with a transfer endorsed thereon or delivered therewith duly executed by the registered holder or by his attorney or successor duly appointed, together with such reasonable assurance or evidence of signature, identification and authority to transfer as the board may from time to time prescribe, upon payment of all applicable taxes and any fees prescribed by the board, upon compliance with such restrictions on transfer as are authorized by the articles and upon satisfaction of any lien referred to in section 7.05.

7.04 Transfer Agents and Registrars. The board may from time to time appoint a registrar to maintain the securities register and a transfer agent to maintain the register of transfers and may also appoint one or more branch registrars to maintain branch securities registers and one or more branch transfer agents to maintain branch registers of transfers, but one person may be appointed both registrar and transfer agent. The board may at any time terminate any such appointment.

7.05 Lien on Shares. The corporation has a lien on any share or shares registered in the name of a shareholder or his legal representative for any debt of that shareholder to the corporation.

7.06 Enforcement of Lien. The lien referred to in the preceding section may be enforced by any means permitted by law and:

(a) where the share or shares are redeemable pursuant to the articles of the corporation by redeeming such share or shares and applying the redemption price to the debt;

Page 9

(b)   subject to the Act, by purchasing the share or shares for cancellation for a price equal to the book value of such share or shares and applying the proceeds to the debt;

(c)   by selling the share or shares to any third party whether or not such party is at arms length to the corporation, and including, without limitation, any officer or director of the corporation, for the best price which the directors consider to be obtainable for such share or shares; or

(d)   by refusing to register a transfer of such share or shares until the debt is paid.

7.07 Share Certificates. Every holder of one or more shares of the corporation shall be entitled, at his option, to a share certificate, or to a non-transferable written acknowledgement of his right to obtain a share certificate, stating the number and class or series of shares held by him as shown on the securities register. Share certificates and acknowledgements of a shareholder's right to a share certificate, respectively, shall be in such form as the board shall from time to time approve. Any share certificate shall be signed in accordance with section 2.02; provided that, unless the board otherwise determines, certificates representing shares in respect of which a transfer agent and/or registrar has been appointed shall not be valid unless countersigned by or on behalf of such transfer agent and/or registrar. A share certificate shall be signed manually by at least one director or officer of the corporation or by or on behalf of the transfer agent and/or registrar. Any additional signatures required may be printed or otherwise mechanically reproduced. A share certificate executed as aforesaid shall be valid notwithstanding that one of the directors or officers whose facsimile signature appears thereon no longer holds office at the date of issue of the certificate.

7.08 Replacement of Share Certificates. The board or any officer or agent designated by the board may in its or his discretion direct the issue of a new share certificate in lieu of and upon cancellation of a share certificate that has been mutilated or in substitution for a share certificate claimed to have been lost, destroyed or wrongfully taken on payment of such fee, not exceeding Three Dollars ($3.00), and on such terms as to indemnity, reimbursement of expenses and evidence of loss and of title as the board may from time to time prescribe, whether generally or in any particular case.

7.09 Joint Shareholders. If two (2) or more persons are registered as joint holders of any share, the corporation shall not be bound to issue more than one certificate in respect thereof, and delivery of such certificate to one of such persons shall be sufficient delivery to all of them. Any one of such persons may give effectual receipts for the certificate issued in respect thereof or for any dividend, bonus, return of capital or other money payable or warrant issuable in respect of such share.

Page 10

7.10 Deceased Shareholders. In the event of the death of a holder, or of one of the joint holders, of any share, the corporation shall not be required to make any entry in the securities register in respect thereof or to make payment of any dividends thereon except upon production of all such documents as may be required by law and upon compliance with the reasonable requirements of the corporation and its transfer agents.

Section Eight

MEETINGS OF SHAREHOLDERS

8.01 Annual Meetings. The annual meeting of shareholders shall be held at such time in each year and, subject to section 8.03, at such place as the board, the chairman of the board, the managing director or the president may from time to time determine, for the purpose of considering the financial statements and reports required by the Act to be placed before the annual meeting, electing directors, appointing auditors and for the transaction of such other business as may properly be brought before the meeting.

8.02 Special Meetings. The board, the chairman of the board, the managing director or the president shall have power to call a special meeting of shareholders at any time.

8.03 Place of Meetings. Meetings of shareholders shall be held at the registered office of the corporation or elsewhere in the municipality in which the registered office is situate or, if the board shall so determine, at some other place in or outside Canada.

8.04 Notice of Meetings. Notice of the time and place of each meeting of shareholders shall be given in the manner provided in section 10.01 not less than twenty-one (21) nor more than fifty (50) days before the date of the meeting to each director, to the auditor and to each shareholder who at the close of business on the record date, if any, for notice is entered in the securities register as the holder of one or more shares carrying the right to vote at the meeting. Notice of a meeting of shareholders called for any purpose other than consideration of the financial statements and auditor's report, election of directors and reappointment of the incumbent auditor shall state the nature of such business in sufficient detail to permit the shareholder to form a reasoned judgment thereon and shall state the text of any special resolution to be submitted to the meeting. A shareholder may in any manner waive notice of or otherwise consent to a meeting of shareholders.

8.05 List of Shareholders Entitled to Notice. For every meeting of shareholders, the corporation shall prepare a list of shareholders entitled to receive notice of the meeting, arranged in alphabetical order and showing the number of shares entitled to vote at the meeting held by each shareholder. If a

Page 11

record date for the meeting is fixed pursuant to section 8.06, the shareholders listed shall be those registered at the close of business on a day not later than ten (10) days after such record date. If no record date is fixed, the shareholders listed shall be those registered at the close of business on the day immediately preceding the day on which notice of the meeting is given, or where no such notice is given, the day on which the meeting is held. The list shall be available for examination by any shareholder during usual business hours at the registered office of the corporation or at the place where the securities register is kept and at the place where the meeting is held.

8.06 Record Date for Notice. The board may fix in advance a record date, preceding the date of any meeting of shareholders by not more than fifty (50) days and not less than twenty-one (21) days, for the determination of the shareholders entitled to notice of the meeting, provided that notice of any such record date is given not less than seven (7) days before such record date, by newspaper advertisement in the manner provided in the Act. If no record date is so fixed, the record date for the determination of the shareholders entitled to notice of the meeting shall be the close of business on the day immediately preceding the day on which the notice is given.

8.07 Meetings Without Notice. A meeting of shareholders may be held without notice at any time and place permitted by the Act:

(a)   if all the shareholders entitled to vote thereat are present in person or represented by proxy or if those not present or represented by proxy waive notice of or otherwise consent to such meeting being held; and

(b)   if the auditors and the directors are present or waive notice of or otherwise consent to such meeting being held.

At such a meeting any business may be transacted which the corporation at a meeting of shareholders may transact.

8.08 Chairman, Secretary and Scrutineers. The chairman of any meeting of shareholders shall be the first mentioned of such of the following officers as have been appointed and who is present at the meeting: president, managing director, chairman of the board or a vice-president who is a shareholder. If no such officer is present within fifteen (15) minutes from the time fixed for holding the meeting, the persons present and entitled to vote shall choose one of their number to be chairman. If the secretary of the corporation is absent, the chairman shall appoint some person, who need not be a shareholder, to act as secretary of the meeting. If desired, one or more scrutineers, who need not be shareholders, may be appointed by a resolution or by the chairman with the consent of the meeting.

8.09 Persons Entitled to be Present. The only persons entitled to be present at a meeting of the shareholders shall be those entitled to vote thereat, the directors and auditors of the corporation and others who, although not entitled to vote, are entitled or required under any provision of the Act or the articles or by-laws to be present at the meeting. Any other person may be admitted only on the invitation of the chairman of the meeting or with the consent of the meeting.

8.10 Quorum. A quorum for the transaction of business at any meeting of shareholders shall be two (2) persons present in person, each being a shareholder entitled to vote thereat or a duly appointed proxy for an absent shareholder so entitled.

8.11 Right to Vote. Subject to the provisions of the Act as to authorized representatives of any other body corporate, at any meeting of shareholders in respect of which the corporation has prepared the list referred to in section 8.05, every person who is named in such list shall be entitled to vote the shares shown thereon opposite his name except, where the corporation has fixed a record date in respect of such meeting pursuant to section 8.06, to the extent that such person has transferred any of his shares after such record date and the transferee, upon producing properly endorsed certificates evidencing such shares or otherwise establishing that he owns such shares, demands not later than ten (10) days before the meeting that his name be included to vote the transferred shares at the meeting. In the absence of a list prepared as aforesaid in respect of a meeting of shareholders, every person shall be entitled to vote at the meeting who at the time is entered in the securities register as the holder of one or more shares carrying the right to vote at such meeting.

8.12 Proxies. Every shareholder entitled to vote at a meeting of shareholders may appoint a proxyholder, or one or more alternate proxyholders, who need not be shareholders, to attend and act at the meeting in the manner and to the extent authorized and with the authority conferred by the proxy. A proxy shall be in writing executed by the shareholder or his attorney and shall conform with the requirements of the Act.

8.13 Time for Deposit of Proxies. The board may specify in a notice calling a meeting of shareholders a time, preceding the time of such meeting by not more than forty-eight (48) hours exclusive of non-business days, before which time proxies to be used at such meeting must be deposited. A proxy shall be acted upon only if, prior to the time so specified, it shall have been deposited with the corporation or an agent thereof specified in such notice or, if no such time is specified in such notice, unless it has been received by the secretary of the corporation or by the chairman of the meeting or any adjournment thereof prior to the time of voting.

8.14 Joint Shareholders. If two (2) or more persons hold shares jointly, any one of them present in person or represented by proxy at a meeting of

Page 13

shareholders may, in the absence of the other or others, vote the shares; but if two (2) or more of those persons are present in person or represented by proxy and vote, they shall vote as one on the shares jointly held by them.

8.15 Votes to Govern. At any meeting of shareholders every question shall, unless otherwise required by the articles or by-laws or by law, be determined by the majority of the votes cast on the question. In case of an equality of votes either upon a show of hands or upon a poll, the chairman of the meeting shall be entitled to a second or casting vote.

8.16 Show of Hands. Subject to the provisions of the Act, any question at a meeting of shareholders shall be decided by a show of hands unless a ballot thereon is required or demanded as hereinafter provided. Upon a show of hands every person who is present and entitled to vote shall have one vote. Whenever a vote by show of hands shall have been taken upon a question, unless a ballot thereon is so required or demanded, a declaration by the chairman of the meeting that the vote upon the question has been carried or carried by a particular majority or not carried and an entry to that effect in the minutes of the meeting shall be prima facie evidence of the fact without proof of the number or proportion of the votes recorded in favour of or against any resolution or other proceeding in respect of the said question, and the result of the vote so taken shall be the decision of the shareholders upon the said question.

8.17 Ballots. On any question proposed for consideration at a meeting of shareholders, and whether or not a show of hands has been taken thereon, any shareholder or proxyholder entitled to vote at the meeting may require or demand a ballot. A ballot so required or demanded shall be taken in such manner as the chairman shall direct. A requirement or demand for a ballot may be withdrawn at any time prior to the taking of the ballot. If a ballot is taken each person present shall be entitled, in respect of the shares which he is entitled to vote at the meeting upon the question, to that number of votes provided by the Act or the articles, and the result of the ballot so taken shall be the decision of the shareholders upon the said question.

8.18 Adjournments. If a meeting of shareholders is adjourned for less than thirty (30) days, it shall not be necessary to give notice of the adjourned meeting, other than by announcement at the earliest meeting that is adjourned. If a meeting of shareholders is adjourned by one or more adjournments for an aggregate of thirty (30) days or more, notice of the adjourned meeting shall be given as for an original meeting.

8.19 Resolution in Writing. A resolution in writing signed by all of the shareholders entitled to vote on that resolution at a meeting of shareholders is as valid as if it had been passed at a meeting of the shareholders unless a written statement with respect to the subject matter of the resolution is submitted by a director or the auditors in accordance with the Act.

Page 14

8.20 Only One Shareholder. Where the corporation has only one shareholder or only one holder of any class or series of shares, the shareholder present in person or by proxy constitutes a meeting.

Section Nine

DIVIDENDS AND RIGHTS

9.01 Dividends. Subject to the provisions of the Act, the board may from time to time declare dividends payable to the shareholders according to their respective rights and interests in the corporation. Dividends may be paid in money or property or by issuing fully paid shares of the corporation.

9.02 Dividend Cheques. A dividend payable in cash shall be paid by cheque drawn on the corporation's bankers or one of them to the order of each registered holder of shares of the class or series in respect of which it has been declared and mailed by prepaid ordinary mail to such registered holder at his recorded address, unless such holder otherwise directs. In the case of joint holders the cheque shall, unless such joint holders otherwise direct, be made payable to the order of all of such joint holders and mailed to them at their recorded address. The mailing of such cheque as aforesaid, unless the same is not paid on due presentation, shall satisfy and discharge the liability for the dividend to the extent of the sum represented thereby plus the amount of any tax which the corporation is required to and does withhold.

9.03 Non-receipt of Cheques. In the event of non-receipt of any dividend cheque by the person to whom it is sent as aforesaid, the corporation shall issue to such person a replacement cheque for a like amount on such terms as to indemnity, reimbursement of expenses and evidence of non-receipt and of title as the board may from time to time prescribe, whether generally or in any particular case.

9.04 Record Date for Dividends and Rights. The board may fix in advance a date, preceding by not more than fifty (50) days the date for the payment of any dividend or the date for the issue of any warrant or other evidence of right to subscribe for securities of the corporation, as a record date for the determination of the persons entitled to receive payment of such dividend or to exercise the right to subscribe for such securities, provided that notice of any such record date is given, not less than fourteen (14) days before such record date, by newspaper advertisement in the manner provided in the Act. Where no record date is fixed in advance as aforesaid, the record date for the determination of the persons entitled to receive payment of any dividend or to exercise the right to subscribe for securities of the corporation shall be at the close of business on the day on which the resolution relating to such dividend or right to subscribe is passed by the board.

Page 15

9.05 Unclaimed Dividends. Any dividend unclaimed after a period of six (6) years from the date on which the same has been declared to be payable shall be forfeited and shall revert to the corporation.

Section Ten

NOTICES

10.01 Method of Giving Notice. Any notice (which term includes any communication or document) to be given (which term includes sent, delivered or served) pursuant to the Act, the regulations thereunder, the articles, the by-laws or otherwise to a shareholder, director, officer, auditor or member of a committee of the board shall be sufficiently given if delivered personally to the person to whom it is to be given or if delivered to his recorded address or if mailed to him at his recorded address by prepaid ordinary or air mail or if sent to him at his recorded address by any means of prepaid transmitted or recorded communication. A notice so delivered shall be deemed to have been given when it is delivered personally or to the recorded address as aforesaid; a notice so mailed shall be deemed to have been given when deposited in a post office or public letter box and shall be deemed to have been received on the fifth day after so depositing; and a notice so sent by any means of transmitted or recorded communication shall be deemed to have been given when dispatched or delivered to the appropriate communication company or agency or its representative for dispatch. The secretary may change or cause to be changed the recorded address of any shareholder, director, officer, auditor or member of a committee of the board in accordance with any information believed by him to be reliable. The recorded address of a director shall be his latest address as shown in the records of the corporation or in the most recent notice filed under the Corporations Information Act, whichever is the more current.

10.02 Notice to Joint Shareholders. If two (2) or more persons are registered as joint holders of any share, any notice shall be addressed to all of such joint holders but notice to one of such persons shall be sufficient notice to all of them.

10.03 Computation of Time. In computing the date when notice must be given under any provision requiring a specified number of days notice of any meeting or other event, the date of giving the notice shall be excluded and the date of the meeting or other event shall be included.

10.04 Undelivered Notices. If any notice given to a shareholder pursuant to section 10.01 is returned on three (3) consecutive occasions because he cannot be found, the corporation shall not be required to give any further notices to such shareholder until he informs the corporation in writing of his new address.

Page 16

10.05 Omissions and Errors. The accidental omission to give any notice to any shareholder, director, officer, auditor or member of a committee of the board or the non-receipt of any notice by any such person or any error in any notice not affecting the substance thereof shall not invalidate any action taken at any meeting held pursuant to such notice or otherwise founded thereon.

10.06 Persons Entitled by Death or Operation of Law. Every person who, by operation of law, transfer, death of a shareholder or any other means whatsoever, shall become entitled to any share, shall be bound by every notice in respect of such share which shall have been duly given to the shareholder from whom he derives his title to such share prior to his name and address being entered on the securities register (whether such notice was given before or after the happening of the event upon which he became so entitled) and prior to his furnishing to the corporation the proof of authority or evidence of his entitlement prescribed by the Act.

10.07 Waiver of Notice. Any shareholder (or his duly appointed proxyholder), director, officer, auditor or member of a committee of the board may at any time waive any notice, or waive or abridge the time for any notice, required to be given to him under any provisions of the Act, the regulations thereunder, the articles, the by-laws or otherwise and such waiver or abridgement shall cure any default in the giving or in the time of such notice, as the case may be. Any such waiver or abridgement shall be in writing except a waiver of notice of a meeting of shareholders or of the board which may be given in any manner.

ENACTED AND PASSED by the board the ....24th...... day of ..January............., 19 8-....

WITNESS the seal of the Corporation.

(apply corporate seal)

John A. Doe
_____   _____
President   Secretary

The foregoing By-Law No. 1 is hereby passed by and consented to by the signatures of all of the directors of the Corporation this .....24th... day of January............., 19 8-........

John A. Doe
_____

_____

The foregoing By-Law No. 1 is hereby confirmed by and consented to by the signatures of all of the shareholders of the Corporation this .....24th... day of .January............., 19 8-....

John A. Doe
_____

_____

c. BANKING ARRANGEMENTS

Unless the articles, general by-law, or the provisions of a unanimous shareholder agreement provide otherwise, the articles are deemed to state that the directors may, without authorization of the shareholders, borrow money on the credit of the corporation; issue, reissue, sell or pledge debt obligations of the corporation; in some circumstances guarantee on behalf of the corporation to secure performance of an obligation of another person; mortgage or otherwise create a security interest in any of the corporation's property in order to secure any obligation of the corporation.

In spite of these inherent borrowing powers, a bank will still require the corporation to pass a borrowing by-law.

Your bank manager will supply you with the by-law, resolution and any other banking papers required to be passed or signed by his or her own bank. The bank will require you to file a copy of the by-law in the printed form supplied by the bank.

The original by-law should be kept in your minute book and signed by all of the directors and shareholders and the copy should be filed with the bank.

The bank will also require you to file with it a banking resolution on the form supplied by it. This resolution will be discussed below. Other forms will be required by your bank, and your bank manager will explain them to you.

You may wish to consider opening an account at a trust company or credit union. Unlike a bank, trust companies and credit unions normally pay interest on chequing accounts. However, if you need financing, a bank is probably your best bet because it will lend money on such security as assignment of accounts receivable, whereas trust companies and credit unions will not. They advance loans mainly on mortgages.

In one of the banking forms you will be appointing "signing authorities." These are the persons empowered to write cheques drawn on the company. The bank will ask that you name the officers empowered with this responsibility.

Usually it is the president alone, or the president and secretary (two signatures required).

You may also want to consider setting up a separate "petty cash" account with wide signing authority (including your secretary) for amounts up to a maximum of $50 or $100.

The main account can then be safely protected while at the same time allowing for the smooth operation of the business.

d. DIRECTORS' RESOLUTIONS

After passing the by-law, the directors should pass resolutions (see Sample #18) to accomplish the following:

(a) Appoint officers. Officers of a corporation are appointed by the board of directors to manage day-to-day affairs of the corporation. The directors may designate the offices of the corporation, appoint officers, specify their duties and delegate powers to them. Two or more offices may be held by the same person. In a one-person corporation, the sole director/shareholder may be responsible for both offices and can function as both president and secretary.

(b) Authorize the issuance of shares.

(c) Approve the share certificates. Share certificates are included in the package available from the publisher. You attach one blank share certificate to the minutes of directors, or resolutions of directors, to establish the form of the share certificate of the corporation.

(d) Adopt the corporate seal. Although this is not mandatory, you may still find occasion to affix the corporate seal to various documents and contracts.

Resolutions of the Director(s) of
John Doe & Associates Limited

BE IT RESOLVED: Allotment of Shares

   1. 100 shares of the Corporation are hereby allotted to John Doe subject to payment therefor in the aggregate amount of $100.00.

   2. The board of directors hereby fixes the sum of $100.00 as the aggregate consideration for the issuance of the said 100 shares.

   3. Upon receipt by the Corporation of payment in full for the said 100 shares, they shall be issued as fully paid and non-assessable and certificates therefor be issued to John Doe or as he may in writing direct.

Form and Execution of Share Certificates

   BE IT RESOLVED that the form of Share Certificates contained in the Minute Book of the Corporation be and the same is hereby approved and adopted as the form of share certificates of the corporation and that share certificates shall be signed by the President and the Secretary, and the common seal of the company affixed thereto by and in the presence of the said officers.

Appointment of Officers

   BE IT RESOLVED that the following persons be and they are hereby elected or appointed officers of the Corporation to hold office during the pleasure of the Board, namely:

President — John Albert Doe
Secretary — John Albert Doe

Adoption of Corporate Seal

BE IT RESOLVED that the seal, an impression of which appears in the margin hereof, is hereby adopted as the corporate seal of the Corporation.

(Note: Press your seal on the side of the page beside this resolution.)

Fiscal Year

BE IT RESOLVED that pursuant to Section 2.01 of By-law No.1 of the by-laws of the Corporation, the director hereby determines that the first fiscal period of the Corporation shall terminate on the 31st day of January, 198- and that thereafter the fiscal year of the Corporation shall terminate on the 31st day of January in each year.

Transfer of Assets

*BE IT RESOLVED that the Corporation purchase the motor vehicle, namely a 1982 Chevrolet, serial number 1234567B89, from John A. Doe, shareholder-director, and that the said purchase be secured by a promissory note.

BE IT RESOLVED that the corporation execute the said promissory note in such manner as required to give full effect to the transactions hereinbefore described.

Appointment of Bank

BE IT RESOLVED that the directors open and maintain a bank account in the corporate name at the Canadian Imperial Bank of Commerce, Yonge & St. Clair Branch, and that a copy of the resolution as to signing officers of the company be annexed to these minutes and the same be adopted as a resolution of the director(s).

The foregoing resolutions are hereby passed by and consented to by the signature of the sole (all) director(s) of the corporation this 24th day of January, 198-.

John A Doe
_____
John Albert Doe

*The Income Tax Act may require you to transfer assets at fair market value. If you are in a situation where such asset transfers create a paper "gain" where you could be liable for capital gains tax you may want to consider making an election under s.85 of the Income Tax Act. This section allows you to defer payment of this tax, but requires a more complicated share structure and the filing out of some government forms. See your accountant or the tax office for further information.

(e) Set fiscal year. A corporation is not restricted to a calendar year for the purpose of its yearly financial statements and may choose any year-end that is convenient.

(f) Appoint a banker and signing officers.

(g) Appoint one or more auditors to hold office until the first annual or special meeting of shareholders.

e. SHAREHOLDERS' RESOLUTIONS

The act directs that auditors must be appointed by the shareholders of the corporation. Generally speaking, the auditors are appointed to inspect or audit the books of the corporation to protect the shareholders' interests. Remember that an auditor is a person who is responsible for matching cheques, bills and receipts with entries in the corporation's books to ensure that everything is done honestly. Your regular day-to-day bookkeeper or an accountant would not be called your auditor.

The act also recognizes the fact that in small closely held corporations an audit is unnecessary as the shareholders are often closely involved in the day-to-day financial affairs of the corporation. The shareholders of corporations that do not offer their securities to the public, have the consent of all the shareholders, and have net assets not exceeding $2 500 000 and gross sales or operating revenues not exceeding $5 000 000 may exempt the corporation from the audit provisions of the act. This written consent must be given each year by the shareholders, usually at the annual general meeting, or in the resolutions passed in lieu of the meeting. Most companies will hire an accountant to give advice on the day-to-day running of the business, but these people need not be appointed in the director's minutes or approved by the shareholders.

Where the size tests of a corporation cannot be met, an exemption from the appointment of an auditor may nevertheless be obtained upon written annual application to the Companies Branch, to be followed by a hearing to ensure that the exemption would not be prejudicial to the public interest.

Samples #19 and #20 show two alternative resolutions relating to the appointment or non-appointment of auditors.

You should see an accountant to ensure that proper financial records are kept and to complete tax and other returns.

SAMPLE #19
SHAREHOLDERS' RESOLUTION APPOINTING ACCOUNTANT

Appointment of Accountant
John Doe & Associates Ltd.

BE IT RESOLVED

that MR. CHARLES BROWN, C.A., be and he is hereby appointed accountant of the Corporation to hold office until the first annual meeting of the shareholders at a remuneration to be fixed by the Board of Directors, the directors being hereby empowered to fix such remuneration.

The foregoing resolution is hereby passed by and consented to by the signature of the sole shareholder of the Corporation this 20th day of January, 198-.

John A. Doe.
_____
John Albert Doe

The undersigned, being the sole shareholder of John Doe & Associates Limited does hereby consent that the Corporation shall be exempt from the provisions of Part XII of the Business Corporations Act, 1982, regarding the appointment and duties of an auditor in respect of the financial year of the Corporation ending January 31, 198-, and in respect of each year thereafter until this consent is revoked.

DATED the 28th day of January, 198-.

John A. Doe.

_____
John Albert Doe

SAMPLE #21
SHAREHOLDERS' RESOLUTION ON REMOVAL OF DIRECTOR

Resolution of the Shareholders of
John Doe & Associates Limited

The following resolution was passed and consented to by all the shareholders of JOHN DOE & ASSOCIATES LTD. at a general meeting called for the purpose of electing and/or removing directors of the corporation.

BE IT RESOLVED

That JOHN A. DOE be removed as a director of the corporation and that JACK B. DOE be appointed to the Board of Directors until the next annual general meeting.

DATED the 28th day of January, 198-.

John A. Doe.

_____
John A. Doe

You will recall that sections 3.03 and 3.04 of our model by-law outlines the procedure for the election of and removal of directors. It states that directors shall be elected and removed yearly at the annual meeting but if this is not done it can be done any time at a special meeting of the shareholders called for that purpose. As mentioned, rarely are these meetings actually held, but one should always take care and prepare the proper resolution to be signed by the shareholders (see Sample #21).

f. COMPLETION OF VARIOUS REGISTERS

Following the issue or transfer of any shares, the appropriate registers should be completed in order to provide a visual summary of the operation.

There are four registers involved and filling them out is quite simple.

1. Shareholders' register

Following the issuance of shares of the corporation to a person who is already a shareholder of the corporation, the shareholders' register should be completed by listing that person's name and the aggregate number of shares of the corporation then held by that person.

If and when there is a transfer, the previous entry of that person's name on the shareholders' register should be ruled out and the new shareholder's name inserted on the next line.

In the event that shares are issued to a person who was not previously a shareholder of the corporation, his or her name should be added to the shareholders' register and the number of shares issued to that person included in the appropriate place.

2. Shareholders' ledger

This simply provides a chronological breakdown of the acquisition, sale and particulars of the shares by each shareholder. The information required is simple and straightforward.

3. Stock transfer register

This simply provides a chronological breakdown of the various transfers of any stock. It does not record the issue of new stock but rather keeps track of it after its initial issue.

4. Directors' register

In this register is entered the name and address of each director, together with his or her office if he or she is appointed an officer, all entered on the date he or she is elected.

When the director retires, his or her retirement date is entered and his or her name may be crossed off the records.

g. THE INITIAL NOTICE AND NOTICE OF CHANGE

Within 60 days of incorporation, you must file an Initial Notice — Form 1 (see Sample #22), which functions like an annual return in that all the pertinent information concerning the corporation is disclosed on it. If any of the information on the Initial Notice becomes outdated, you are required to file an amended notice within 10 days of the change.

If any section of the form is not applicable to your situation, put N/A or Not Applicable in the blanks. Forms which have sections left blank will be returned as incomplete. No fee is payable for filing either the Initial Notice or Notice of Change. If you have a change in directors at your annual meeting, you will file a Notice of Change showing the new names and addresses.

This form is available from the Ministry of Consumer and Commercial Relations. The Ministry will mail you an Initial Notice if you phone and ask for it. To fill out the form, follow the instructions for each numbered section.

1. Set out the name of the corporation exactly as it appears on your Certificate of Incorporation.

2. The incorporation number, as it appears on your Certificate of Incorporation, is listed here.

3. The date of incorporation as set out on the Certificate of Incorporation is needed here.

4. Here you would put "by Certificate."

5. State the full, complete address of the registered office. This means giving the suite number if the office is located in a multi-suite building; the postal code; and the municipality or post office designation for the area in which the office is located. A post office box number is not acceptable.

6. If the address of your principal place of business is different from your head office, put it here.

7. Give full names of current directors (no initials). Place a check mark

under Yes or No, whichever is appropriate. The full residential address, like head office address, must be disclosed. Post office box numbers are not acceptable. Give the apartment number, street number, rural route number and municipality or post office and postal code. The date indicated should be the most recent date the person named became a director. If you have too many directors to fit in the space provided (which is unlikely with a small private corporation), attach a schedule to the Initial Notice (or Notice of Change). Label it "Schedule A", and place the name and number of the corporation at the top of it.

8. State the full names (no initials) of all officers. A president and secretary are generally inserted (the shareholder of a one-person company usually holds both offices). Full residential addresses are also required. Give suite numbers and postal codes — not post office box numbers. The full date, including the day and the month on which the person named became an officer of the corporation should also be set down.

9. Put N/A here, unless there has been a change in the directors of the corporation, in which case you would fully set out the names and addresses of those people who stopped being directors and set out the date on which they ceased to act as directors.

10. Again you would put N/A here, unless there was a change in officers, in which case list the full

name and address of those who no longer act as officers.

Sample #22 illustrates a typical Initial Notice. You can see how it is to be altered in the event of a Notice of Change.

All incorporation forms that are not supplied by the publisher may be obtained by calling the Companies Branch information office at (416) 596-3761 and asking for the form by name and number. As you can see, the Initial Notice or Notice of Change is Form 1.

h. ONTARIO CORPORATIONS TAX QUESTIONNAIRE

Once you are incorporated, your obligation to pay corporate tax begins. Therefore, you should fill out the Ontario Corporation Tax Questionnaire and mail it to the Ministry of Revenue. If you do not fill out the questionnaire, you will receive all the tax forms and notices at your residential address, as set out in Article 4 of your Articles of Incorporation. As this can be a nuisance, you should complete and mail the questionnaire at the same time you prepare your Initial Notice.

An example of a completed Ontario Corporations Tax Questionnaire is shown in Sample #23. You can obtain a copy of this form by contacting —

Ministry of Revenue
Corporations Tax Branch
P.O. Box 622
33 King Street W.
Oshawa, Ontario
L1H 8H6
Telephone: Oshawa (416) 433-6666
              Toronto (416) 965-1160
                            ext. 6666

SAMPLE #22
INITIAL NOTICE — FORM 1

Ontario — Ministry of Consumer and Commercial Relations / Ministère de la Consommation et du Commerce

Companies Branch / Direction des Compagnies

Form 1 - Corporations Information Act
Formule 1 - Loi sur les renseignements exigés des compagnies et associations

NOTE/REMARQUE: 1. Check appropriate box at right/Cocher la case pertinente à droite.
2. All items below must be answered/Prière de remplir toutes les rubriques ci-dessous.
3. Return form to/Renvoyer à la: Examination and Notice Section, Companies Branch
Ministry of Consumer and Commercial Relations
Ministère de la Consommation et du Commerce
Section des examens et des avis, Direction des compagnies

☒ Initial Notice/ Avis Intial
OR/OU
☐ Notice of Change/ Avis de modification

1. Corporation Name/Dénomination sociale de la compagnie ou de l'association	2. Ontario Corporation Number/Numéro matricule de la compagnie ou de l'association en Ontario
John Doe & Associates Limited	12345

3. Date of incorporation, amalgamation or continuation / Date de constitution, de fusion ou de prorogation	4. Manner of incorporation, amalgamation or continuation / Mode de constitution, de fusion ou de prorogation
15 01 85 (day/jour month/mois, year/année)	By certificate

5. Full Address of Registered or Head Office/Adresse complète du siège social

Suite 007, 390 Bay Street, Toronto, Ontario

Postal Code / Code postal: Z 1 P 0 G 0

6. Principal Place of Business if different from Registered or Head Office/Établissement commercial principal s'il est différent du siège social

N/A

Postal Code / Code postal

7. Present Directors Full Names / Noms et prénoms des administrateurs actuels	★Canadian Resident / Résident canadien: Yes Oui / No Non	Full Residence Address / Adresse personnelle au complet	Date Elected Director / Date de l'élection de l'administrateur
John Albert Doe	✓	204-415 Eglinton Ave. Toronto, Ontario Z1P 0G0	Jan. 15, 1985

8. Present Officers' Full Names / Noms et prénoms des dirigeants actuels	Full Residence Address / Adresse personnelle au complet	Date Appointed Officer / Date de nomination du dirigeant
President/Président John Albert Doe	204-415 Eglinton Ave. Toronto, Ontario Z1P 0G0	Jan. 15, 1985
Secretary/Secrétaire John Albert Doe		
Treasurer/Trésorier		

9. Full names of persons who, since last notice, have been but are no longer directors/Noms et prénoms des personnes qui depuis le dernier avis étaient administrateurs mais ne le sont plus	Full Residence Address / Adresse personnelle au complet	Date Ceased to be Director / Date de cessation

10. Full names of persons who, since last notice, have been but are no longer officers/Noms et prénoms des personnes qui depuis le dernier avis étaient dirigeants mais ne le sont plus	Full Residence Address / Adresse personnelle au complet	Date Ceased to be Officer / Date de cessation

I/Je soussigné, **John Albert Doe**
(Print name in full/Écrire le nom au complet en caractères d'imprimerie)
certify that the information herein contained is true and correct/atteste que les renseignements précités sont véridiques et exacts.

Signature ▶ *John Albert Doe*

▼ Check appropriate box/Cocher la case pertinente
☑ Director/Administrateur
☐ Officer/Dirigeant
☐ Other person having knowledge of the affairs of the Corporation/Autre personne au courant des affaires de la compagnie ou de l'association

07200 (06/85)

★ Applies only in case of corporation with share capital
Ne remplir que s'il s'agit d'une compagnie à capital social

☐ **See Deficiency Notice on reverse side**
Voir l'Avis de renseignements complémentaires ▶

Ontario Corporations Tax Questionnaire

Ministry of Revenue / Corporations Tax Branch

Ontario

Your co-operation in completing and returning this questionnaire will enable the Ministry of Revenue to provide you with the forms, information and other services regarding your obligations under the Corporations Tax Act. On completion, please return to:

Ministry of Revenue
Corporations Tax Branch
P.O. Box 622
33 King Street West
Oshawa, Ontario L1H 8H6

Telephone: Oshawa (416) 433-6666
Toronto (416) 965-1160 ext. 6666

Please type or print in BLOCK CAPITAL letters

Corporation Name (in full)	Ontario Corporation Number
JOHN DOE AND ASSOCIATES LTD.	123456

Date of Incorporation/Amalgamation	Date of Corporation's First Taxation Year End*	Jurisdiction
Day 2 3 / Month 1 / Year 8 —	Day 3 0 / Month 1 / Year 8 8	Ontario

Name of Person Enquiries Should be Directed to	Telephone Number
JOHN A. DOE	(416) 123-4567

Full Mailing Address	
SUITE 5600 390 BAY STREET	
TORONTO ONTARIO	Postal Code Z 1 P 0G 0

* The first taxation year cannot exceed fifty-three weeks from the date of incorporation. If the period chosen by you exceeds this limit, a separate Corporations Tax Return must be filed for the period commencing with the date of incorporation and ending on the day preceding the start of the adopted taxation year whether or not the corporation is active.

I certify that the information herein contained is true and correct

Print Name in Full	Signature	
JOHN A. DOE	John A. Doe	☒ Director ☒ Officer ☐ Other person having knowledge of the affairs of the corporation

6

HOW TO ISSUE, CANCEL, AND TRANSFER SHARES

a. INTRODUCTION

The issuing and cancelling of shares is a relatively simple affair because the form of share certificate is already prepared for you. You should be careful, however, to distinguish in your own mind the initial issues out of treasury, i.e., from the unissued "pool," and simple transfers from one person to another where no new shares are issued. They all involve different operations. Fortunately, the simplest operation comes first.

The following points should be noted regarding shares generally:

(a) For the average small, private corporation a relatively few share certificates will suffice for normal purposes. This is because there are normally only a few shareholders and each share certificate can represent the total number of shares held by each person. (You do not need a separate certificate for each share.)

(b) Share certificates should, whenever possible, remain with the minute book because if they are sent to the individual shareholder, some will inevitably be lost and you will then be faced with the annoying problem of replacing lost share certificates.

(c) Share certificates have to be issued under the seal of the company and signed by two officers.

(d) Share certificates should be numbered consecutively in the space provided at the top of the certificate.

(e) You can see the remaining information that is needed by looking closely at the share certificates in Samples #24 and #25.

(f) To cancel shares, simply write the word "cancelled" across the face of the certificate and staple it shut on top of the tab or stub of the certificate (see Sample #25).

(g) You must be sure to follow the procedure outlined in Article 8 of your Articles of Incorporation which will specify the restrictions on the issuing or transferring of shares. For example, if your restriction is that, before an allotment or transfer is effective, it must be passed by the majority of the board of directors, then you must prepare the appropriate directors' minutes. Don't forget that you may draft whatever restrictions you want under this section, but whatever the restriction is it must be complied with.

b. SUBSEQUENT ISSUE OF SHARES

The initial issue of shares is generally conducted during the organization procedure of the corporation, and was explained in chapter 5.

The main reason why a small, non-public corporation would want to issue additional shares is to bring in a new "partner."

The reasons for this may be either financial or because the new partner is, or will be, a major factor in the running of the business.

Whatever reason, shares issued to a new "partner" serve to psychologically "lock" the partner into the business and allow him or her to share in the increase in net worth of the business.

SAMPLE #24
COMPLETED SHARE CERTIFICATE

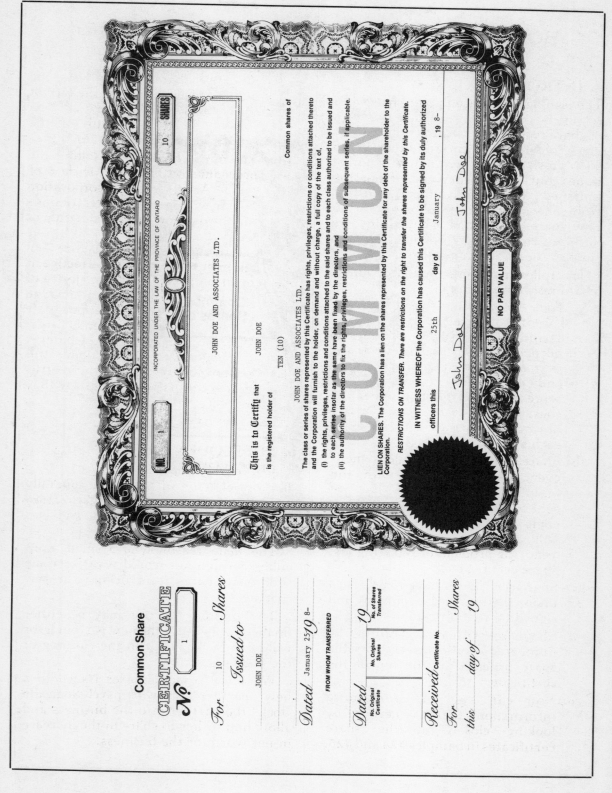

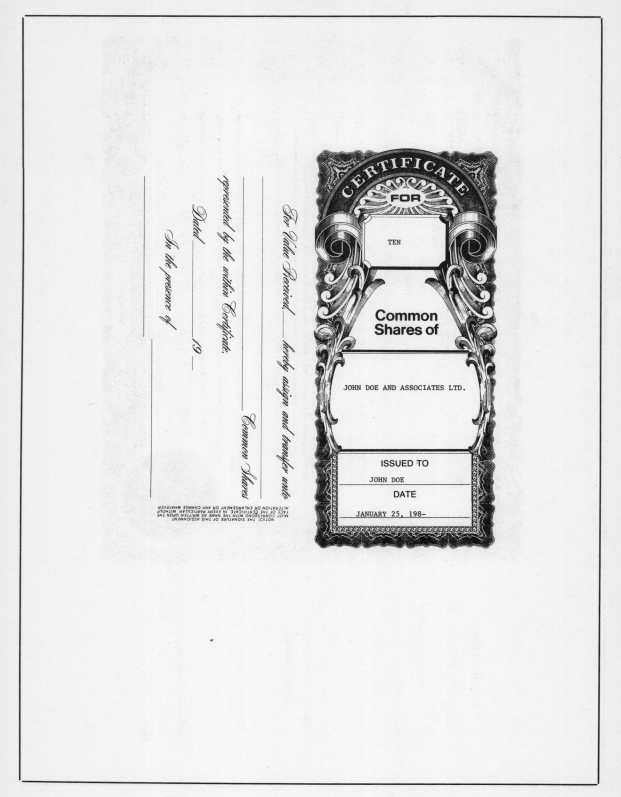

SAMPLE #25
CANCELLED SHARE CERTIFICATE

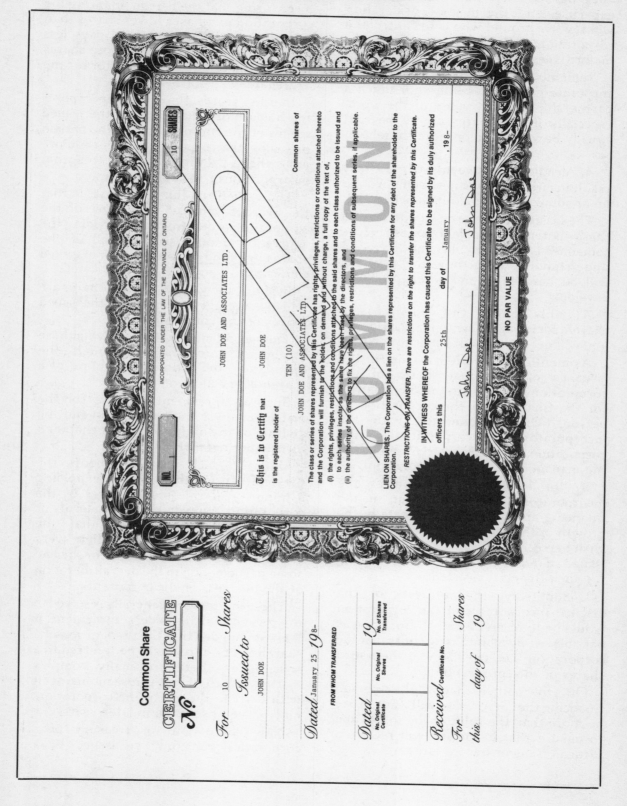

If the reason for bringing in a new "partner" is to gain management expertise, etc., the major consideration will revolve around who is to control the corporation and have the deciding vote on major issues.

Remember, despite the existence of the corporate entity, it is still very much a partnership in every sense of the word, especially if the shares are to be split equally between two or more shareholders.

A "deadlock" between partners may result in either the business being wound up or someone buying out someone else.

The lesson here is to be sure to discuss these potential problem areas before someone is brought in and have an understanding about how the situation will be handled if and when problems develop.

At this point the need for a shareholders' agreement may arise and you will need to consult a solicitor on this.

As mentioned, another reason for the issuance of additional shares of the corporation would be to provide security for the financing of the corporation by persons closely connected with the incorporator or incorporators of the corporation, but not directly involved in the management of the corporation.

If, for example, a relative of the incorporator wished to assist in the financing and possibly participate in the growth of the corporation, he or she may wish to receive a certain percentage of the issued shares of the corporation in return for such financial assistance.

Undoubtedly, the interests of the original incorporator of the corporation would be to receive as much financing as possible, while maintaining control of the corporation (i.e., over 50% of the issued shares of the corporation).

On the other hand, the person financing the corporation will want to pay no more than the value of the shares and to ensure that he or she will receive a return on his or her investment.

These conflicting interests are generally resolved in a new corporation by ensuring that the person financing the corporation purchases fewer shares than the original incorporator and pays less money for the aggregate of those shares than did the original incorporator for the aggregate of his or her shares.

In other words, the original incorporator holds more than 50% of the issued shares of the corporation and the person financing the corporation pays no more per share than did the original incorporator of the corporation.

The reason for this, of course, is that the average value of each share of the corporation is determined by dividing the aggregate amount paid for all of the shares by the aggregate number of issued shares.

In short, the value for which shares are issued is averaged among all of the issued shares of the corporation.

The second method for resolving these conflicting interests is through the negotiation and ultimate execution of a shareholders' agreement.

Such an agreement provides for the management of the corporation and the division of any of its profits (see chapter 8 for further details).

Without such an agreement, the person financing the corporation holding a minority of the issued shares of the corporation would have no legal or practical way of ensuring that the corporation paid dividends if there were earnings or of ensuring that he or she had some participation in the overall direction of the business of the corporation.

These matters are generally resolved in the form of a shareholders' agreement. It is recommended that the preparation of a shareholders' agreement be referred to a solicitor as there are many complex matters which, if not foreseen and dealt with early in the life of the corporation, may prove unsolvable in later years.

New shares out of treasury of a corporation can only be issued by a resolution of the board of directors of the corporation.

If the board of directors of the corporation decides to issue new shares in the corporation, it must determine the number of shares to be issued and the worth for which the shares are to be issued.

If the shares are not issued for money but are issued for assets or past services, the board of directors must specify in its resolution the value of such assets or the value of such past services to the corporation.

The board of directors should always have in mind that if the shares are issued by the corporation for a value less than the true value of the shares, the effect of such issuance is to decrease the average value of every issued share of the corporation.

Correspondingly, by issuing shares for a value greater than their true value, the average value of every issued share of the corporation increases.

Thus, considerable care should be taken by the board of directors in determining the value for which shares of the corporation will be issued.

Sample #26 shows the resolutions of a board of directors issuing shares of the corporation either for money or assets.

c. TRANSFER OF SHARES

The most important thing to remember when transferring shares from one person to another (this is not the same as issuing new shares out of treasury) is that you must follow the requirements set out in Article 8 of your Articles of Incorporation.

In other words, whatever restrictions you have on transfer must be noted and the procedure followed as set out.

For example, if your restriction on transfer is that a majority of the board of directors must approve the transfer, a director's resolution stating this must be prepared (see Sample #27).

The next step is to physically write the word "cancelled" diagonally across the face of the old certificate, complete the transfer form on the back and then fold it up and staple it to the stub so that the face of it is not conspicuous. This serves to clearly indicate that the share certificate is cancelled and not missing.

Finally, you complete a new certificate in the same manner as the old one, taking care, of course, to insert the new owner's name and new certificate number.

RESOLUTIONS OF THE DIRECTOR(S) OF
JOHN DOE & ASSOCIATES LTD.

BE IT RESOLVED THAT:

1. Fifty (50) shares of the Corporation (hereinafter called the "common shares") are hereby allotted subject to payment therefor to Jane Doe for $15 000;

2. The Board of Directors hereby fixes the sum of $15 000 as the aggregate consideration for the issuance of the said fifty (50) common shares;

3. Upon receipt by the Corporation of payment in full for the said fifty (50) common shares, the said common shares be issued as fully paid and non-assessable and certificates therefor be issued to the respective allottees, or as they may in writing direct.

OR

WHEREAS the Corporation has agreed with Jane Doe to purchase her 1982 Ford Van truck, registration no. XB1234, owned by Jane Doe in consideration of the issuance and allotment of fifty (50) fully paid and non-assessable shares of the Corporation;

RESOLVED that:

1. The directors hereby affix a fair market value in the sum of $5 000 as the consideration for which fifty (50) shares of the Corporation may be allotted and issued;

2. The directors hereby determine by this express resolution that the Ford Van referred to above is in all the circumstances of the transaction the fair equivalent of $5 000;

3. Fifty (50) shares of the Corporation are hereby allotted to Jane Doe;

4. The said shares are issued as fully paid and non-assessable shares and the proper officers of this Corporation are hereby authorized to issue and deliver certificates for such shares to Jane Doe upon receipt by this Corporation of conveyances and transfers of the said vehicle to the Corporation.

The foregoing resolution(s) are hereby passed and consented to by the signature of the director(s) of the corporation this 25th day of January, 198-.

John A. Doe

_____
John A. Doe

RESOLUTIONS OF THE DIRECTOR(S) OF
JOHN DOE & ASSOCIATES LTD.

BE IT RESOLVED THAT:

    1. Ten (10) shares of the corporation registered in the name of John Doe and evidenced by share certificate no. 1 be transferred to Jane Doe.

    2. Share certificate no. 2 for ten (10) shares be issued to Jane Doe and that the transfer as set out be duly recorded on the share registry of the corporation.

    The foregoing resolutions are hereby passed and consented to by the signature of the director(s) of the corporation this 25th day of January, 198-.

John A. Doe
_____
John A. Doe

7

TRANSFERRING ASSETS INTO A NEW CORPORATION

Once your corporation is incorporated and organized, the next step is for your company to acquire assets. The assets it acquires can be purchased in the normal course of business with cash that is in the company bank account. However, any assets of your proprietorship or partnership that has now been incorporated are generally transferred into the corporation.

Incorporation may simplify accounting. For example, it is easier for the corporation to own assets and deduct depreciation and operating expenses rather than each shareholder owning them and renting them to the corporation. Otherwise both the corporation and the shareholders would have to keep records of the assets and corresponding rental payments.

However, you should remember that after the transfer, the assets become the property of the corporation and are subject to seizure by creditors of the corporation.

If you want to minimize your risk of loss, you may transfer certain assets into the corporation that are necessary for carrying on business and retain other assets, like your car, in your own name and lease them to the corporation. As a result, if the business enterprise fails, these assets would not be subject to seizure.

a. FEDERAL INCOME TAX CONSIDERATIONS

In the absence of certain provisions in the Income Tax Act, which will be discussed shortly, transfers or property between persons not dealing at arm's length (like you and your corporation) must take place at fair market value, which could result in the triggering of a gain (either income or capital) or the recapture of capital cost allowance. If the parties are not dealing at arm's length, the transferor will be deemed to have received proceeds of disposition equal to the fair market value of the property transferred, and the transferee will be deemed to have acquired the assets at that value even though no consideration was paid or received.

For example, assume that you purchased a car for $10 000 for your proprietorship, and over a couple of years you depreciated the car on the books down to $6 000. You then incorporate and transfer the car into the corporation at a deemed price of its fair market value of say, $11 000. You would have to include $4 000 in your personal income, being the amount of the recaptured depreciation, plus a further $666 taxable capital gain, being two-thirds of the capital gain realized.*

b. SECTION 85 ROLLOVER

In order to eliminate the onerous tax consequences that have just been described, section 85 of the Income Tax Act permits you and the corporation to *elect* for income tax purposes that the transfer take place at a price agreed upon by the parties, so that any gain or recapture that would otherwise arise on the transfer at fair market value will be deferred. The elected amount becomes the proceeds of disposition of the property to the transferor and the cost of the property to the transferee corporation.

---

*As of December, 1987, two-thirds of all capital gains incurred by a taxpayer in 1988 and 1989 must be included in income. After 1989, three-quarters of all gains must be included in income.

In the example above, the elected amount for the car could be $6 000, which is the undepreciated amount in the proprietorship's books. Accordingly there would be no tax consequence to the vendor, and the car would appear on the corporation's books at $6 000.

There are certain requirements in section 85 of the Income Tax Act for the transfer of assets into the corporation to occur at an amount other than the fair market value of the assets. These requirements are as follows:

(a) The corporation to which the assets are transferred must be a taxable Canadian corporation (i.e., a corporation resident in Canada when the transfer takes place and continuously since June 18, 1971 or incorporated in Canada). It is not necessary for the transferor to be a resident of Canada, and can be an individual, partnership, trust, or other corporation.

(b) The transferor and transferee must make a joint election of the transfer price, on a form prescribed by the government, at other than fair market value.

(c) The transferor must receive some share consideration for the transfer (one or two shares of the transferee corporation is enough). The balance of the consideration can be non-share consideration, like a promissory note or other form of security, but to avoid income tax consequences should not be equal to an amount greater than the cost for tax purposes of the capital item being transferred. To determine the cost for income tax purposes you should consult your professional advisors.

(d) The property being transferred must be depreciable or non-depreciable capital property, eligible capital property like goodwill, inventory other than real property, or resource property. Real property that is capital property, or an option in real property owned by a non-resident of Canada does not qualify as property that can be transferred under section 85.

In determining what amount to elect for the transfer price, certain rules apply as follows:

(a) The elected amount cannot exceed the fair market value of the property transferred.

(b) The elected amount cannot be less than the fair market value of the non-share consideration received by the transferor.

(c) Where the elected amount exceeds the fair market value of the property transferred, or is less than the fair market value of the non-share consideration received, the elected amount is set at that fair market value.

c. PROVINCIAL TAX CONSIDERATIONS

It is equally important to consider the application of Ontario or other provincial retail sales tax to a transaction like the one described above.

The transfer of assets into a newly incorporated corporation is exempt from retail sales tax if, at the time of the transfer, the transferor and his or her direct lineal family (e.g., son or daughter) own 95% of the outstanding shares and if the assets have not previously been exempted from sales tax under a similar rollover. For other provinces, consult your professional advisors.

In other words, if you are transferring assets to a corporation of which you are the sole shareholder, retail sales tax need not be paid. But this exemption applies only once. If you try to transfer the same assets from the new corporation to another corporation, sales tax must be paid.

The same situation applies in the case of a partnership provided the partners retain the same proportionate interest in the newly incorporated company as they had in the partnership.

d. COMPLETING THE TRANSFER OF ASSETS

Once you have elected the amount at which the assets are to be transferred and have filled out the appropriate government forms, you should prepare documents to indicate that actual title to the assets has passed to the corporation.

For example, where a motor vehicle is being transferred, make sure that the usual government transfer forms are filled out and registered. Also, any car insurance policies should be transferred into the name of the corporation.

It is advisable to prepare and execute a bill of sale of the assets transferred and keep it with the minute book of the corporation. In some cases, it may be necessary to register the bill of sale.

Where accounts receivable are being transferred, all those persons who owed the proprietorship or partnership money should be contacted and informed to make payment to the corporation.

Finally, the directors of the corporation should hold a meeting authorizing the transfer of assets to the corporation and the election of the purchase price. This resolution should be documented in the minutes of the corporation.

Because transactions like the one described can be complex, it is recommended that you seek the advice of your accountant and lawyer to ensure that all the steps are completed properly.

e. FINANCING THE TRANSACTION

As mentioned above, when an asset is sold to a corporation, it must give something back in return as consideration for the transfer and under Section 85, this consideration must include some share consideration. The share consideration may be combined with non-share consideration, the simplest form of which is the demand promissory note (see Sample #28). Promissory note forms can be picked up at any stationery store.

A note like this should be executed on behalf of the corporation in favor of each party transferring assets to the corporation if non-share consideration is appropriate under the circumstances.

You will note that under the terms of the note, John Doe is entitled to "demand" payment at any time. You may wonder what is to stop Mr. Doe from demanding payment immediately.

First, he is not likely to demand payment unless there are sufficient funds in the corporation's bank account to pay him, and he is in the best position to know whether or not he can collect, particularly when in most instances he is the sole shareholder.

Second, if he had to sue, it would be tantamount to suing himself since he is also the part owner of the "entity."

Third, to demand whole of payment would be contradictory to the formation of the corporation.

So, you see, a demand note payable to a shareholder-director of an incorporated partnership is in a relatively safe position. Usually an informal agreement between the working "partners" as to where and when the notes should be presented for payment is sufficient.

Interest payments made to the holder of the note are taxable in his or her hands. The principal amount due the holder is not, as it is analagous to repayment of a loan made to the corporation.

There is one risk that is taken when transferring assets to a corporation. If the company should go bankrupt or have judgments registered against it, the assets may be subject to seizure by the trustee in bankruptcy or the judgment creditor. In the case of the debt owed to you by the corporation, it would be relegated to general creditor status and you would share in the proceeds of the resale of the assets along with the other creditors.

This happens infrequently because you can usually foresee these events for some time before they occur and make demand on your note and collect on it.

SAMPLE #28
DEMAND NOTE

$1 999   March 30, 198-

ON DEMAND after date I promise to pay to the order of John Doe at Toronto, Ontario, one thousand nine hundred and ninety-nine dollars ($1 999) with interest at the rate of ten (10%) percent per annum, as well after as before maturity, FOR VALUE RECEIVED.

JOHN DOE & ASSOCIATES LTD.

Seal   Per:

John A. Doe

———————————————
President

Where there is a transfer of numerous and valuable assets, extra precaution is usually taken in the form of a security agreement or a chattel mortgage given by the corporation to the transferor. This elevates the transferor or shareholder to the secured creditor status and entitles him or her to a higher ranking if there is claim on the assets.

In this case, it is recommended that a solicitor be consulted as a chattel mortgage needs to be properly drafted and registered to be effective.

8

DO YOU NEED A SHAREHOLDERS' AGREEMENT?

Once your corporation is incorporated and organized, and any licences required by your company have been obtained, you are ready to start business. As your business grows, if there is more than one shareholder, you should consider implementing a shareholders' agreement.

A shareholders' agreement is an agreement entered into by some, and generally all, the shareholders of a corporation to establish the course of future conduct in a variety of areas. These may include:

(a) The right of a shareholder to nominate a director or directors

(b) The appointment of officers of the corporation

(c) The right of shareholders to compete, or the obligation not to compete, with the corporation

(d) The pro rata right of shareholders to participate in future offerings of the corporation

(e) Restrictions or prohibitions on the transfer of shares

(f) The right or obligation of shareholders or the corporation to purchase the shares of a shareholder upon the occurrence of an event (e.g., irreconcilable differences of opinion, or the death or permanent disability of a shareholder), together with a formula for valuation of the shares to be purchased, and the mechanism for purchase

(g) Mechanisms for the resolution of disputes

Of the above features, those most commonly seen in shareholders' agreements are (a), (d) and (e). The remaining features appear with varying frequency, depending upon the business involved and the circumstances surrounding the shareholders. In any event, it is important to note that a shareholders' agreement should be drafted as simply as possible. The more complex the agreement the more likely is the possibility of it being unworkable.

Consider, now, the most common features in a shareholders' agreement, and why such provisions are important.

a. RIGHT TO NOMINATE A DIRECTOR

Where there is no shareholders' agreement, a corporation is managed by its board of directors, and the board is elected by the shareholders. In small closely held corporations, where there are only one or two shareholders, the directors are often shareholders as well. This generally assures each person that he or she will be involved in the management. As a result, the shareholders' agreement would not necessarily require the representation of each shareholder on the board since each would be a director.

However, a shareholder having a minority interest in the corporation would want to be assured that he or she, or someone he or she chooses, is a director. This is generally accomplished through an agreement. Otherwise the majority shareholders woud be free to select the directors of their choice.

b. PRO RATA RIGHTS AND OBLIGATIONS

When most new companies are started, each of the original shareholders generally invests a nominal amount to get the company going and looks to bank financing or future potential profits for growth and capitalization. The shareholders may simply agree that each will be responsible for his or her pro rata share of future financing requirements through the purchase of more shares if other methods of financing are not readily available or practical. Problems may arise when one of the shareholders is unwilling to purchase the pro rata share of the future offering; the remedies available to the remaining shareholders can be sought mainly through a shareholders' agreement.

This type of situation deals with the *obligation* of a shareholder to participate in future offerings; it is equally important to protect a shareholder's *right* to participate. Consider a situation where a corporation has two shareholders, one having a majority of shares and the other a minority interest. The majority shareholder may issue a large number of shares to himself or herself, thereby diluting the equity base and decreasing the minority shareholder's overall interest in the corporation. Accordingly, shareholders' agreements generally contain a pro rata right to participate in future offerings of securities, and require that no more securities may be offered without the prior approval of, say, two-thirds or three-quarters of the holders of the common shares.

c. RESTRICTIONS ON THE TRANSFER OF SHARES

Unlike public corporations where there can be a wide variety of shareholders, the shareholders of private companies are often few in number and wish to restrict the admission of any new partners into their organization. As a result, however, the marketability of the shares may be affected.

These conflicting considerations, namely the restriction on admission of new partners and the marketability of shares, are often resolved by the use of a "right of first refusal" clause in a shareholders' agreement.

A shareholder wishing to sell shares with this technique must first offer to sell the shares to the other shareholders. If the remaining shareholders do not accept the offer, the offeror is entitled to sell the shares to a third party at a price and on terms not more favorable than those contained in the offer to the remaining shareholders. If the selling shareholder

cannot find a buyer and is required to amend the original offer, the procedure must be repeated.

d. BUY-SELL PROVISIONS

Shareholders' agreements may contemplate the purchase by a shareholder of the shares of another shareholder, upon the happening of a certain event. This event is most commonly restricted to the death of the shareholder.

The death of a shareholder in a private corporation carries serious implications for both the deceased's estate and the remaining shareholders. As already mentioned, the shares of a private company generally have a limited market value so that the personal representative of the deceased's estate may have some difficulty in disposing of them.

The surviving shareholders suddenly have a new partner whom they did not choose; namely, the deceased's personal representative. If the personal representative decides not to sell the deceased's shares to the remaining shareholders, these shareholders may encounter difficulties in managing the corporation should the personal representative take an active part in the day-to-day management of the corporation.

Therefore, many shareholders agreements contain buy-sell provisions whereby the estate of the deceased shareholder would sell, and the surviving shareholders would purchase, all of the shares of the deceased at a specified price or at a price to be determined under the agreement. The buy-sell provisions should cover the following points:

(a) How the purchase is to be funded
(b) How the shares are to be valued to establish a purchase price

Funding the purchase of shares is not a problem for those shareholders with sufficient personal wealth to either pay the purchase price or to persuade a banker to lend them the money. However, it is more common to accomplish funding through business life insurance policies on the lives of all the shareholders.

The corporation may be the beneficiary to which the insurance proceeds go, or the surviving shareholders may receive the proceeds directly. Tax consequences vary with the manner in which the insurance policy is implemented, so you should consult your insurance representative, accountant, and lawyer before proceeding with an insurance funding program.

The valuation of shares to establish a purchase price is often difficult, and no simple solution exists. However, the following techniques are often used:

(a) A fixed amount in the agreement

(b) A formula approach, usually book value, adjusted book value, multiple of earnings, or a combination of assets and earnings

(c) Appraisal by an independent third party such as the corporation's auditors or a business valuator

(d) Annual agreement among the shareholders

(e) A combination of any or all of the above

e. KEEP IT SIMPLE

Shareholders, usually with the best intentions in mind, often instruct their lawyers to draft shareholders' agreements. Once the agreement is executed it is stored with the corporate files and forgotten for years. When a situation arises requiring guidance from the agreement, such as the provisions relating to the purchase of shares, the shareholders are often dismayed to realize that the agreement is far too complicated and cumbersome to carry out its intent, and because of the passage of time, its provisions are out of date.

Therefore, I recommend that you seek professional advice from your accountant and lawyer before engaging in the negotiation and execution of a shareholders' agreement. Most important, make sure that you keep it simple!

The form of shareholders' agreement shown as Sample #29 is a very simple one. It is enclosed for your information only, and legal advice should be sought for further assistance.

AGREEMENT made this 25th day of October, 198-.

BETWEEN:

JOHN DOE, of the Town of Anytown, in the Province of Ontario

(hereinafter "DOE")

OF THE FIRST PART

— and —

JACK GREEN, of the Town of Anytown, in the Province of Ontario

(hereinafter "GREEN")

OF THE SECOND PART

— and —

JOHN DOE & ASSOCIATES LIMITED, a corporation incorporated pursuant to the laws of the Province of Ontario

(hereinafter the "Corporation")

OF THE THIRD PART

WHEREAS the authorized capital of the Corporation is to be divided into an unlimited number of common shares;

AND WHEREAS Doe beneficially owns 501 common shares and Green beneficially owns 499 common shares, being all the common shares issued and outstanding;

AND WHEREAS Doe and Green (hereinafter collectively referred to as the "SHARE-HOLDERS") desire to provide for the constitution, organization, management and supervison of the Corporation, and for the disposition and succession of the common shares thereof;

NOW THEREFORE, in consideration of the mutual covenants and agreements herein contained and subject to the terms and conditions hereinafter set out, the parties hereto agree as follows:

1.00 CONSTITUTION

1.01   The Corporation shall not:

a) Amend its Articles of Incorporation;
b) Make an arrangement;
c) Amalgamate;
d) Apply to a jurisdiction other than the Dominion of Canada for an instrument of continuation;

pursuant to the Business Corporations Act, 1982 except upon the unanimous consent of the Shareholders.

1.02   The Corporation shall not pass, amend, or recind any by-law of the Corporation, except upon the unanimous consent of the Shareholders.

1.03   The Corporation shall not:
a) Redeem; or
b) Purchase for cancellation any of the Shares of the Corporation;

nor shall it sanction or approve any:
c) Conversion;
d) Surrender;
e) Allotment;
f) Transfer

of the shares of the Corporation, except upon the unanimous consent of the Shareholders, or as hereinafter provided.

2.00 DIRECTORS

2.01.   The Board of Directors shall manage or supervise the management of the affairs and business of the Corporation.

2.02   The Board of Directors of the Corporation shall consist of a minimum of one and a maximum of three directors. The initial Board of Directors shall consist of three directors and shall include one nominee of Doe and one nominee of Green. The third director shall be elected by the unanimous vote of the shareholders. The number of directors within the minimum and maximum range may be increased or decreased only upon the unanimous consent of the shareholders. If the Board is increased to four directors, then the Board shall consist of two nominees of Doe and two nominees of Green. If the Board of Directors is increased to five directors the Board shall consist of two nominees of Doe and two nominees of Green, and the fifth director shall be elected by the unanimous consent of the shareholders.

2.03.   A quorum for the transaction of business at meetings of the Board of Directors shall consist of a majority of the directors.

2.04   Except as otherwise provided in this Agreement, all questions proposed for consideration of the Board of Directors at any Board meeting shall, in the presence of a quorum, be determined by a majority of the directors in attendance; provided however, that the affirmative vote of at least one nominee director of Doe and one nominee director of Green shall be required to decide any action of the Board of Directors.

3.00 ISSUE OF SHARES

3.01 **Pro Rata Offering**

a) Except as the parties shall otherwise unanimously agree in writing, no shares shall be issued by the Corporation unless, and each offering by the Corporation of shares shall be made, in accordance with paragraph 3.01.

b) Each offer shall be made to the shareholders as nearly as may be in proportion to the number of shares respectively held by them at the date of the offer.

c) Every offer shall be made in writing and shall state that a party which desires to subscribe for shares in excess of its proportion shall, in its subscription specify the number or amount, as the case may be, of shares in excess of its proportion that it desires to purchase. If a shareholder does not subscribe for its proportion, the unsubscribed shares shall be used to satisfy the subscription of the other shareholder for the shares in excess of its proportion. No shareholder shall be bound to take any shares in excess of the amount it so desires.

3.02 **Unsubscribed shares** If all of the shares of any issue are not subscribed for within a period of 45 days after the same are offered to the parties pursuant to the provisions of paragraph 3.01, the Corporation may, during the next three months, offer and sell all or any of the shares not taken up by the parties but the price at which shares may be allotted and sold shall not be less than the subscription price offered to the parties pursuant to paragraph 3.01 and on terms more favorable than those offered to the parties.

3.03. **Additional Parties** Every issue of shares shall be subject to the condition that the subscriber therefor shall, if not a party hereto, agree to be bound by the terms of this agreement.

4.00 DISPOSITION OF SHARES

4.01 **Purchase Rights** If any shareholder (the "Offeror") desires or is required by law to transfer any of his shares to another person, or to sell or dispose of any shares, the other shareholder (the "Offeree") shall have the prior right to purchase the shares on the terms and in accordance with the procedure contained in paragraph 4.02.

4.02 **Procedure on Transfers**

a) An Offeror shall notify the Corporation in writing of his desire or intention to transfer, sell or otherwise dispose of any shares. The notice (the "Selling Notice") shall set out:

(i) the number and a brief description of each class of shares;
(ii) the price and terms of payment which the Offeror is willing to accept for the shares; and
(iii) if the Offeror has received an offer to purchase the shares, the name and address of the potential purchaser and the terms of payment and price contained in this offer.

b) The shares shall then be offered to the Offeree on the terms of payment and for the price contained in the Selling Notice, and shall remain open for acceptance as hereinafter provided for a period of 45 days.

c) If, within that period the Offeree does not agree to purchase all of the shares offered, he shall be deemed to have refused to purchase the shares offered, and the Offeror may offer and sell all of the shares offered to any other person at the price and on the terms and conditions set out in the Selling Notice.

d) If all of the shares offered shall be accepted by the Offeree, the shares shall be sold to him for the price and on the terms contained in the Selling Notice.

4.03 **Additional Parties** Every transfer of shares shall be subject to the condition that the purchaser thereof shall, if not a party hereto, agree to be bound by the terms of this agreement.

4.04   Release from Liability If a sale, transfer or other disposition is completed in accordance with this Article, the Offeror shall upon completion of the purchase be absolved from all liability to or in respect of the Corporation whether under the provisions of this agreement or under any guarantee, indemnity or other financial assistance given in respect of the operations in the Corporation arising after the date of sale, transfer or other disposition and the purchaser of the shares offered shall assume all obligations in respect thereof.

5.00   GENERAL

5.01   a)   This Agreement may be terminated upon:

   (i)   written notice from one of the shareholders to the other;
   (ii)   the bankruptcy or insolvency of either party;
   (iii)   the enactment of any legislation requiring the dissolution of the Corporation or rendering its continued operation illegal.

   b)   The Corporation shall thereupon be dissolved unless where termination occurs pursuant to paragraph 5.01(a)(i), one of the shareholders agrees to purchase the shares of the other upon terms and conditions that they mutually agree.

5.02   Assignment This agreement is not assignable by any party except insofar as its benefit and burden pass with equity securities transferred in accordance with the agreement. This agreement shall enure to the benefit of and be binding upon the heirs, executors, administrators, successors, or any other legal representatives of the parties hereto.

5.03   Additional Parties Every issue and transfer of shares shall be subject to the condition that each subscriber or transferee, as the case may be, shall, if not a party hereto, agree to be bound by the terms hereof and become a party hereto by executing an agreement to be bound hereby.

5.04   Miscellaneous

   a)   The Shareholders shall not sell, assign, transfer, mortgage, charge, pledge or hypothecate their shares except pursuant to the terms hereof or except upon the unanimous consent of the shareholders.

   b)   In the event of any conflict between the terms of this agreement and the Articles of Incorporation and By-laws of the Corporation, the terms of this agreement shall prevail and the parties hereto shall forthwith cause such necessary alterations to be made to the Articles of Incorporation and By-laws as are required so as to resolve the conflict.

5.05   Third Party Payments Any arrangements made by the parties hereto with third parties and all payments to third parties are the responsibility of the party entering into such arrangement and not of the other party.

   IN WITNESS WHEREOF the parties hereto have executed this Agreement as of the date first above mentioned.

SIGNED, SEALED and DELIVERED
      in the presence of

_____

JOHN DOE

_____

JACK GREEN

JOHN DOE & ASSOCIATES LIMITED

Per: _____

9

RUNNING YOUR CORPORATION SMOOTHLY

a. ANNUAL GENERAL MEETING

All corporations are required to hold an annual general meeting of shareholders no later than 18 months after the date of incorporation. All subsequent general meetings must be held 15 months after the preceding meeting. The annual meetings are held at such place in or outside Ontario as the directors determine, or at the registered office of the corporation, subject to any other designation in the articles or a unanimous shareholders' agreement. For example, if the articles or a unanimous shareholders' agreement provide for holding a meeting at a place outside of Ontario, then the meetings can be held at that particular place.

The act provides that at least 10 days' and not more than 50 days' notice of the meeting is required in the case of shareholders in a private corporation. In most cases, formal notice provisions are not required, as the shareholders are notified orally and may waive the notice informally by appearing at the meeting or formally by entering the waiver in the minutes of the meeting.

1. Common items dealt with at a meeting

In a small private corporation the Business Corporations Act, 1982 provides that a financial statement for the period from incorporation or from the last annual general meeting to a date not more than six months before the present meeting is to be laid before the shareholders at the meeting.

The financial statements shall include at least a balance sheet, a statement of retained earnings, an income statement, and a statement of changes in financial position. If the corporation has appointed an auditor, an auditor's report must also

be given. By-laws and resolutions passed by the directors in the previous year are ratified.

Other business that is usually conducted is the appointment of directors and the appointment of auditors, if the shareholders do not waive the appointment.

2. Why hold a meeting?

The annual general meeting also provides a useful opportunity to go over the business and allow those shareholders who perhaps do not take an active part in the business to make their contribution (or complaints).

If you decide not to formally hold an annual general meeting, you may have all the shareholders consent in writing to all the resolutions that could or would normally be passed at a formal meeting (see Sample #30). Many small companies find this a more convenient way to go about the business of holding an annual general meeting.

b. ALL ABOUT SHAREHOLDERS AND DIRECTORS

The following summary of the rights and responsibilities imposed on directors and shareholders is really for your information only. If the relationships in a small, closely held corporation deteriorate to such an extent that these rights are exercised, the corporation would probably cease being effective from a business point of view. However, by reading this section over carefully you will gain a better idea of what is expected of shareholders and directors.

1. Your rights as a shareholder

At one time all shareholders' rights were contained in the body of cases that formed the common law. Now, the trend is to codify these rights in the act that governs companies in each province. The following sections discuss the major parts of the Ontario Business Corporations Act, 1982.

(a) Oppressive and prejudicial conduct

The book, *Palmer on Company Law*, says:

> It has always been the law that if a majority acts in oppression of the minority, the latter may petition the court to wind up the company, on the grounds that it is just and equitable to do so.

This remedy is for wrongs done to a shareholder, creditor, director or officer, and *not* wrongs done to the corporation. In order to wind up the corporation under section 206 of the Business Corporations Act, 1982, you must show that there are grounds to wind up the corporation because the affairs of the corporation are conducted in an oppressive manner. What conduct is oppressive depends on the facts of each case. You, the applicant, will have to tell the court the type of conduct you are complaining about (e.g., "share dilution" or the sale of the major business and assets of the corporation without proper shareholder approval).

The court will exercise its discretion in determining if the application for the winding up order is made for honest reasons, and if such a step would be in the best interests of the corporation.

Frequently this remedy is not effective because the real assets of the corporation consist of the skill, knowledge and business acumen of the directors and/or shareholders, not physical assets with a high retail value. So this type of remedy may not be a remedy at all for the oppressed shareholder since the benefit of these intangible items is lost when the corporation is broken up and its assets sold.

Furthermore, courts have been reluctant to order a winding up of a corporation, so that aggrieved shareholders have been left with little recourse to enforce their personal rights. Therefore, a shareholder may apply to the court for an order the court thinks fit in the circumstances, including the following:

(a) an order restraining the conduct complained of

(b) an order appointing a receiver

(c) an order directing an issue or exchange of shares

(d) an order appointing new directors

(e) an order directing the corporation to purchase the shares of a particular shareholder

(f) an order compensating the aggrieved person

(g) an order winding up the corporation

(b) Derivative actions on behalf of the corporation

As in the previous section, the concern here is with the right of a shareholder, who is generally a minority (i.e., those controlling less than 50% of the voting shares), to bring an action on behalf of the corporation or any of its subsidiaries, when the corporation is being damaged and the directors and officers have not started legal proceedings to protect it.

Because it is really the corporation that is suffering the harm, theoretically the corporation, via the directors, should be the entity that brings the action. However, the minority in this case cannot get the board of directors to take the necessary steps, so the minority shareholders are forced to sue as representatives of the corporation.

To permit an action to be started the court must be satisfied that —

(a) the directors of the corporation or its subsidiary will not bring, diligently prosecute or defend or discontinue the action,

(b) the person applying to the court is acting in good faith,

(c) it appears to be in the best interest of the corporation or its subsidiary that the action be brought, and

SAMPLE #30
RESOLUTIONS OF ANNUAL GENERAL MEETING

In lieu of the 198- Annual General Meeting of the Corporation, the following resolutions are consented to in writing by all the shareholders of the Corporation entitled to attend and vote at an Annual General Meeting of the Corporation, as evidenced by their signatures hereto.

ELECTION OF DIRECTORS
Resolved: John Albert Doe be elected director of the Corporation until the next Annual General Meeting of the Corporation.

APPROVAL OF ACTS OF DIRECTORS AND OFFICERS OF THE COMPANY
Resolved: That all of the acts, contracts, by-laws, resolutions, proceedings and payments made, done and taken by the Directors and Officers of the Corporation since Incorporation of the Corporation be and the same are hereby approved, ratified and confirmed.

FINANCIAL STATEMENTS
Resolved: That the financial statements of the Corporation to January 30, 198- are hereby approved.

WAIVER OF APPOINTMENT OF AUDITOR
The undersigned, being all the shareholders of the Corporation, hereby consent that the Corporation shall be exempt from the provisions of Part XII of the Business Corporations Act, 1982 regarding the appointment and duties of an auditor in respect of the financial year of the Corporation ending January 31, 198-.

Resolved: That the Corporation hereby waive the appointment of an auditor for the corporation for the present fiancial year, pursuant to Part XII of the Business Corporations Act, 1982.

Resolved: That Mr. Charles Brown, C.A. be and he is hereby appointed accountant of the Corporation to hold office until the next annual meeting or until a successor is appointed at a remuneration to be fixed by the directors, the directors being authorized to fix such remuneration, and the Secretary is hereby directed to give the Corporation's accountant written notice of his appointment.

The foregoing resolutions are hereby passed as of the 14th day of June, 198-.

John Doe.

John Albert Doe

Being all the Members of the Corporation.

(d) the person applying to the court has given 14 days' notice to the directors of his or her intention to apply to the court.

After hearing the application, the court may make any order it thinks fit, including:

(a) An order authorizing the person applying, or any other person, to control the conduct of the action

(b) An order giving directions for the conduct of the action

(c) An order directing that any amount payable from a defendant in the action be paid directly to the shareholders and former shareholders

(d) An order requiring the corporation to pay the shareholder's legal fees incurred in connection with the action

(c) Rights of dissenting shareholders

The right to dissent can be exercised by the members of a small, closely held private corporation when the directors and/or majority shareholders propose major changes which materially affect the nature of minority shareholders' investment. Basically this provision allows a shareholder to demand that the corporation purchase his or her shares at fair market value under certain conditions of dissent. All of the following events entitle a shareholder of a private corporation to dissent under this provision:

(a) When a shareholder has dissented on a corporate resolution approving certain amendments to the articles, amalgamations, sale of all or substantially all of its property.

(b) If there has been a compulsory acquisition of shares after acquirer has received 90% of the shares via takeover bid, holders of the remaining 10% of the shares may be forced to sell their shares and demand "fair value" from the acquirer.

(c) If 90% of the shares of the corporation are acquired by one person, holders of the remaining 10% may demand "fair value" for their shares from the corporation.

(d) When there is a termination of shareholdings in a "going private" transaction.

The procedures for a shareholder to dissent and invoke this appraisal right vary depending upon whether the right is triggered by a fundamental change under situation (a) above or under a compulsory acquisition under (b) and (c).

Complex rules provide for a voluntary settlement of fair value followed by procedures for seeking the court's assistance.

This right may not be much help, however, if the corporation is insolvent, as all corporations are prohibited from purchasing shares if the purchase or redemption of their own shares would make them bankrupt or unable to meet their debts as they become due.

(d) The right to requisition a meeting

The holders of not less than 5% of the issued shares which carry the right to vote at a shareholders' meeting may requisition the directors to call a meeting. The purpose of the meeting must be stated in the requisition.

The corporation must reimburse the requisitionist for expenses as long as he or she acted in good faith in the interests of the shareholders.

The court may requisition a shareholders' meeting if a shareholder or director applies to the court. The meeting must be conducted in the manner the court directs.

2. Shareholders' liabilities

One of the advantages of being incorporated is "limited liability," but there are times when this limited liability is not applicable. When the stated capital of the corporation is reduced, each person who was a shareholder on the date of the reduction is individually liable to the corporation's creditors for the amount of money paid to them as a result of the reduction.

To the extent that a unanimous shareholders' agreement restricts the powers of the directors to supervise the management of the business, the directors are relieved of that liability and each shareholder assumes that liability.

If the corporation is dissolved and its property distributed to the shareholders, each shareholder is liable to a claimant of the corporation to the extent of the amount received by the shareholder.

Furthermore, it is common for banks and other lending institutions to obtain a personal guarantee from the directors or shareholders of the corporation before they will lend money to the corporation. If you personally guarantee a loan to your corporation, you are liable as guarantor for the repayment of the loan to the lender.

3. Directors' rights and duties

All private, closely held corporations require a minimum of one director. (Public, distributing corporations require a minimum of three).

The number of directors can be fixed in the Articles of Incorporation or can be a minimum and maximum. The corporation may amend its articles to increase or decrease the fixed number or the minimum and maximum.

Where the articles provide for a minimum and maximum number of directors, the number of directors to be elected is decided from time to time by a special resolution. The corporation must file a certified copy of the special resolution with the Companies Branch within 10 days after it is passed.

A properly completed Notice of Change must also be filed. A majority of the directors must be resident Canadians.

All directors must be of sound mind, not bankrupt, and 18 years of age or older.

In order to conduct business at a meeting of directors, a majority of those present at the meeting must be resident Canadians. A director can be considered present at a meeting if he or she communicates with the other directors by telephone.

Of course you may avoid having meetings by having resolutions drawn up and circulated to all of the directors for their signatures.

Directors are responsible for conducting the business affairs of the corporation. Directors, and the officers they hire, are required to act honestly and to exercise the skill and care of a reasonably prudent person in carrying out their duties. The following is a brief summary of some of the other duties imposed upon directors by the Ontario Business Corporations Act, 1982.

(a) Duty of disclosure

Basically the object of this provision is to prevent directors from making a personal profit to the detriment of the corporation. A director who has a material personal interest in a contract that is important to the corporation is obliged to disclose the nature and extent of his or her interest in the contract to the other directors at the first meeting in which the contract is discussed. After the nature and extent of the director's interest is disclosed, he or she is required to abstain from voting and is not to be considered in the quorum of directors.

If the director's interest in the transaction arises after the transaction is first discussed, he or she must inform the other directors at the next meeting.

If a director fails to make a disclosure in the fashion described, he or she may have the contract ratified by the shareholders by special resolution, if the director acted honestly and in good faith, the transaction was fair and reasonable, and disclosure is made to the shareholders.

A director would be wise to do this because the shareholder approval would allow him or her to keep any personal profit that might otherwise have to be returned to the corporation.

Where a director has not disclosed an interest in a contract, the corporation or a shareholder may apply to the court for an order setting aside the contract or transaction, and directing that the director account to the corporation for any profit or gain realized.

(b) The duty to keep informed

Directors are liable to creditors and, in certain circumstances, to the corporation if they authorize —

    (a) financial assistance to a shareholder, director, officer, or employee

    (b) the purchase, redemption or acquisition of its shares,

    (c) the payment of a commission, or

    (d) the payment of a dividend, and

by reason of these expenditures the corporation is unable to meet its debts as they become due.

Every director and officer must act honestly and in good faith in the best interests of the corporation and exercise the care and diligence of a reasonably prudent person in comparable circumstances.

A director may avoid liability for a resolution if his or her dissent is recorded in the minutes of the meeting in which the resolution was passed. If he or she was not present at the meeting in which the resolution giving rise to the liability was passed, then the director can file a dissent within seven days of becoming aware of the resolution. He or she can also send this dissent to the corporation by registered mail.

This liability is one of the major reasons why directors who are not actively involved in the day-to-day operation of the corporation should carefully read a financial statement and keep in touch with the corporation's accountant. The problem of ignorance of the true state of corporate affairs is less likely to arise in well run small corporations than it is in large, loosely organized corporations.

All incumbent directors are entitled to see financial statements and corporate records at any reasonable time. Retired directors can look at financial records for the period in which they held office.

(c) Liability for wages

Directors are jointly and severally liable for the unpaid wages of employees of the corporation. The maximum amount the directors are liable for is six months' wages and vacation pay accruing for up to twelve months. A director must be sued for the debt within six months after collection proceedings against the corporation proved ineffective. The suit must be brought against the director while he or she is acting as a director or within six months of his or her retirement. The Ontario Ministry of Labour is very efficient at helping employees quickly process wage claims, so this liability is not something to be treated lightly.

All directors of newly formed corporations should keep this responsibility in mind before they sign up as an incorporator or before consenting to act as a director.

(Incorporators and those who sign consent forms are directors until the shareholders officially appoint directors for the corporation.)

4. Directors' indemnification

Directors are entitled to benefit from liability insurance taken out on their behalf by the corporation. This money may be used to indemnify directors and officers from liability for costs, charges, and expenses sustained in a law suit against the director, or against the corporation, for acts done or permitted by him or her in the execution of the duties of the office.

However, the purchase of insurance policies is not a foolproof way of protecting yourself as a director. No corporation is entitled to indemnify a director whom a court has found to be dishonest or in breach of a duty.

A further consideration is that for most small, new corporations, the premiums on insurance policies for the directors may be prohibitively high.

5. Appointment and removal of directors

All directors may be appointed by either signing the Articles of Incorporation as first directors, or by being elected by the shareholders in a general meeting in accordance with the by-laws of the corporation. The people named as first directors in the Articles of Incorporation act as directors until others are elected by the shareholders. Directors may hold office for a term expiring not later than the third annual meeting of shareholders after they were elected. The length of term may be specified in the by-laws. At the end of the term of office, the director may be re-elected.

The shareholders may vote a director out of office at any time by calling a special meeting for the removal of the director, and passing an ordinary resolution for the removal of the director.

If there has been a change in the people who are directors, either at a specially called meeting, or at the annual general meeting, a Notice of Change must be filed indicating the names and addresses of the people who are now directors and the names and addresses of those who left the position.

Officers of the corporation may be dismissed at any time by an ordinary resolution of the directors at a directors' meeting. A dismissal by the directors, however, does not prevent an officer from relying on a contract of employment with the corporation and either being paid a sum in settlement for wrongful dismissal, if such is the case, or suing the corporation for breach of contract.

10

HOW TO CHANGE YOUR CORPORATE NAME

After you have been operating for a number of years you may come to the conclusion that the name "Slipshod Industries Ltd." is not really for you.

Perhaps your name no longer reflects what you do. For example, you may no longer produce silver jewellery exclusively, and customers may be deterred, by reason of the increased interest in gold jewellery, from looking at products supplied by Sam the Silversmith Ltd. Or, you may have incorporated with your own name and now regret it as you get midnight telephone calls from stranded motorists who are able to trace your personal phone from a name like Marvin Mechanic's Towing Services Ltd.

Finally, you may feel a little uncomfortable with a name like North End Appliance Repairs now that you do business and operate out of the south end of town.

These are only a few of the many reasons there are for changing your corporate name. Whatever your reason is, it is simple to change your name in Ontario by amending your articles under section 167 of the Business Corporations Act, 1982. Of course, the tedious name clearance procedure for the new name must be completed before your articles may be amended (see chapter 3). However, once this is done, you may purchase the Articles of Amendment (Form 3) from your local stationer and fill it out in a manner similar to Sample #31.

As you can see from Sample #31, the Articles of Amendment are simple to complete for the purposes of changing your corporate name.

First, you have to pass a special resolution authorizing the change of name. The special resolution should be recorded in the minutes of a special meeting. The manner in which the articles of the Corporation are amended is set out in Paragraph 4 of the Articles of Amendment, which are filed in duplicate.

A fee of $100 payable to the Treasurer of Ontario must accompany your Articles of Amendment. If you pay by cheque, write the name of your corporation on the face of the cheque.

You do not avoid legal liabilities by changing your corporate name. All debts and obligations incurred by the company in its old name remain the responsibility of the company even if it has a new name.

The definition of a special resolution from the Business Corporations Act, 1982 is reproduced for your convenience below:

1(1)43. "special resolution" means a resolution that is

(i) submitted to a special meeting of the shareholders of a corporation duly called for the purpose of considering the resolution and passed, with or without amendment, at the meeting by at least two-thirds of the votes cast, or

(ii) consented to in writing by each shareholder of the corporation entitled to vote at such a meeting or his attorney authorized in writing;

The special resolution should be filed in the minute book. In most small closely held corporations a special resolution is usually passed by having all of the shareholders sign it or consent in writing to the resolution changing the corporate name.

TRANS CODE

C

18

ARTICLES OF AMENDMENT
STATUTS DE MODIFICATION

Form 3
Business
Corporations
Act,
1982

*Formule
numéro 3
Loi de 1982
sur les
compagnies*

1. The present name of the corporation is: *Dénomination sociale actuelle de la compagnie:*

J	O	H	N		D	O	E		&		A	S	S	O	C	I	A	T	E	S		L	I	M	I	T	E	D

2. The name of the corporation is changed to (if applicable): *Nouvelle dénomination sociale de la compagnie (s'il y a lieu):*

P	E	R	S	O	N	A	B	L	E		P	E	R	S	O	N	N	E	L		L	T	D.

3. Date of incorporation/amalgamation: *Date de la constitution ou de la fusion:*

15 JANUARY 198–

(Day, Month, Year)
(jour, mois, année)

4. The articles of the corporation are amended as follows: *Les statuts de la compagnie sont modifiés de la façon suivante:*

To change the name of the Corporation to Personable Personnel Ltd.

(Continued)

109

SAMPLE #31 — Continued

5. The amendment has been duly authorized as required by Sections 167 and 169 (as applicable) of the Business Corporations Act.

La modification a été dûment autorisée conformément à l'article 167 et, s'il y a lieu, à l'article 169 de la Loi sur les compagnies.

6. The resolution authorizing the amendment was approved by the shareholders/directors (as applicable) of the corporation on

Les actionnaires ou les administrateurs (le cas échéant) de la compagnie ont approuvé la résolution autorisant la modification

29   AUGUST   198–
(Day, Month, Year)
(jour, mois, année)

These articles are signed in duplicate.

Les présents statuts sont signés en double exemplaire.

JOHN DOE & ASSOCIATES LIMITED
(Name of Corporation)
(Dénomination sociale de la compagnie)

By/Par: _John A. Doe_
(Signature)
(Signature)
(Description of Office)
(Fonction)

JOHN ALBERT DOE – PRESIDENT

11

HOW TO DISSOLVE YOUR CORPORATION

If you decide that you no longer want to carry on business as a corporation, you may apply to the Companies Branch to dissolve it. For example, your corporation may have been inactive for several years and you wish to rid yourself of the annual paperwork required in filing corporate tax returns. Or, you and the other owners may wish to retire and you are unable to find someone to take over the business.

In order to dissolve a corporation, the shareholders must either —
   (a) *all* agree to the dissolution in writing (see Sample #32), or
   (b) pass a special resolution in favor of dissolution at a shareholders' meeting.

The written consent must be obtained from all the shareholders who would have been entitled to vote at a meeting.

Alternatively, a corporation may be dissolved upon the authorization of all its incorporators at any time within two years of its date of incorporation if the corporation has not commenced business and has not issued any shares.

Before the Articles of Dissolution can be filed, several other matters must be taken care of.

A Notice of Intention to Dissolve (Sample #33) must be published once in the Ontario *Gazette* and once in a newspaper having general circulation in the area where the corporation had its principal place of business in Ontario, or if it does not have a place of business in Ontario, where it has its registered office.

You must also obtain a Certificate of Consent from the Corporations Tax Branch in Toronto. This must accompany your Articles of Dissolution when they are sent in. The Certificate of Consent is valid for 60 days from the date of issuance, so that you should make sure you file your Articles of Dissolution within that period.

You should also get a Clearance Certificate from Revenue Canada indicating that all federal corporate taxes are paid. Contact your local Revenue Canada tax office.

Before dissolving your corporation, you must also pay all debts owing or have your creditors consent to the dissolution (see Sample #34). Any debts payable to unknown creditors may be paid to the Public Trustee.

All corporation filings with the Companies Branch must also be brought up to date.

Now the assets of the corporation can be distributed rateably to all of the shareholders. "Rateable distribution" means a distribution according to the interests of the shareholders in the corporation, i.e., related to the number of shares, promissory notes, and dividends owing to them. All the shareholders can enter into an agreement concerning the disposal of any remaining assets.

Once all these requirements are met, you file the Articles of Dissolution in duplicate (see Sample #35). For a corporation that has started business and issued shares, or has been in existence for more than two years, the articles must be signed by an officer or a director, and the signatures must be originals, not photocopies.

Articles of Dissolution must be accompanied by a written consent to the dissolution from the Corporations Tax Branch, Ministry of Revenue (Ontario).

File these papers with the Companies Branch of the Ministry of Consumer and Commercial Relations. Once the Certificate of Dissolution is issued by the Minister, your corporation no longer exists.

You should advise all tax departments, city assessment and licensing offices that your corporation is dissolved, and that your corporation's last filing with them is final. This helps tie up loose ends.

SAMPLE #32
RESOLUTION FOR DISSOLUTION

BE IT RESOLVED THAT:

1. The Corporation be dissolved pursuant to Section 236 of the Business Corporations Act, 1982.

2. As incidental to the foregoing, the property of the Corporation be distributed rateably among the shareholders of the Corporation according to their rights and interests in the Corporation.

3. The directors and officers are hereby authorized and directed to do, sign and execute all things, deeds, and documents necessary or desirable for the due carrying out of the foregoing.

The foregoing resolution is hereby consented to by all the shareholders of the Corporation pursuant to the Business Corporations Act, 1982 as evidenced by their respective signatures hereto this 20th day of October, 198—.

John A. Doe.

_____

(sole shareholder)

SAMPLE #33
NOTICE OF INTENTION TO DISSOLVE

NOTICE OF INTENTION TO DISSOLVE
JOHN DOE & ASSOCIATES LIMITED

NOTICE IS HEREBY GIVEN that JOHN DOE & ASSOCIATES LIMITED intends to dissolve pursuant to The Business Corporations Act, 1982.

DATED at Toronto this 20th day of October, 198-.

John Doe.

Secretary

SAMPLE #34
CONSENT OF CREDITORS TO DISSOLUTION

CONSENT OF CREDITORS TO DISSOLUTION

TO: <u>JOHN DOE & ASSOCIATES</u> LIMITED

The undersigned being a creditor of the Corporation hereby consents to its dissolution pursuant to Section 237 of THE BUSINESS CORPORATIONS ACT, 1982.

DATED the 20th day of October, 198-.

Cameron Creditor

SAMPLE #35
ARTICLES OF DISSOLUTION

1

For Ministry Use Only
À l'usage exclusif du ministère

Ontario Corporation Number
Numéro de la compagnie en Ontario

444444

Trans
Code

C
18

Stat.

D
28

ARTICLES OF DISSOLUTION
STATUTS DE DISSOLUTION

Form 10
Business
Corporations
Act,
1982

*Formule
numéro 10
Loi de 1982
sur les
compagnies*

1. The name of the corporation is: *Dénomination sociale de la compagnie:*

J	O	H	N		D	O	E		&		A	S	S	O	C	I	A	T	E	S		L	I	M	I	T	E	D

2. Date of Incorporation/Amalgamation   *Date de la constitution ou de la fusion:*

         15   JANUARY   1978

(Day, Month, Year)
(jour, mois, année)

3. The dissolution has been duly authorized under clause 236(a) or (b) (as applicable) of the Business Corporations Act.

    La dissolution de la compagnie a été dûment approuvée aux termes de l'alinéa 236 (a) ou (b) (le cas échéant) de la Loi sur les compagnies.

4. The corporation has
   (A) ~~No debts, obligations or liabilities;~~
   (B) Duly provided for its debts, obligations or liabilities in accordance with subsection 237 (3) of the Business Corporations Act;
   ~~or~~
   (C) ~~Obtained consent to its dissolution from its creditors or other persons having interests in its debts, obligations or liabilities.~~

    La compagnie, selon le cas:
    (A) N'a ni dettes, ni obligations, ni passif;
    (B) A pourvu à ses dettes, à ses obligations ou à son passif conformément au paragraphe 237 (3) de la Loi sur les compagnies;
    (C) A obtenu de ses créanciers ou des autres intéressés à ses dettes, ses obligations ou son passif, le consentement à sa dissolution.

5. After satisfying the interests of creditors in all its debts, obligations and liabilities, if any, the corporation has
   (A) ~~No property to distribute among its shareholders, or~~
   (B) Distributed its remaining property rateably among its shareholders according to their rights and interests in the corporation or in accordance with subsection 237(4) of the Business Corporations Act where applicable.

    Après avoir désintéressé tous ses créanciers s'il y a lieu, la compagnie, selon le cas:

    (A) N'a plus de biens à répartir entre ses actionnaires;

    (B) A réparti les biens qui lui restaient entre ses actionnaires au prorata de leurs droits dans la compagnie ou conformément au paragraphe 237 (4) de la Loi sur les compagnies, s'il y a lieu.

6. There are no proceedings pending in any court against the corporation.

    Aucune instance n'est en cours contre la compagnie.

114

2

7. The corporation has given notice of its intention to dissolve by publication once in the Ontario Gazette and once in

| La compagnie a donné avis de son intention de se dissoudre en publiant un avis à cet effet une fois dans la Gazette de l'Ontario et une fois dans

"   "The Toronto Flyer"   "

a newspaper having general circulation in the place where the corporation has its principal place of business or its registered office (as applicable).

un journal généralement lu à l'endroit où est situé l'établissement principal ou le siège social de la compagnie (selon le cas).

8. The corporation has obtained the consent of the Corporations Tax Branch of the Ministry of Revenue to the dissolution and has filed all notices required under the Corporations Information Act.

La direction de l'impôt des compagnies du Ministère du Revenu a approuvé la dissolution de la compagnie. La compagnie a déposé tous les avis requis par la Loi sur les renseignements exigés des compagnies et associations.

These articles are signed in duplicate.

Les présents statuts sont signés en double exemplaire.

JOHN DOE & ASSOCIATES LIMITED
(Name of Corporation)
(Dénomination sociale de la compagnie)

By/Par: *John A. Doe*
(Signature)   (Description of Office)
(Signature)   (Fonction)

JOHN A. DOE - PRESIDENT

For Ministry Use Only
À l'usage exclusif du ministère

Ontario Corporation Number
Numéro de la compagnie en Ontario

444444

12

REGISTRATION OF OUT-OF-PROVINCE CORPORATIONS

a. CANADIAN CORPORATIONS

If your company was incorporated under the laws of a province other than Ontario, or incorporated federally, you may carry on any business in Ontario or hold land in Ontario without obtaining a licence to do so.

The only requirement is to file an Initial Notice within 60 days of beginning business activities in Ontario. An extra-provincial or federal corporation must file Initial Notice Form 2 (see Sample #36).

On the Initial Notice Form 2, you must state the corporation name, the name under which the corporation will do business in Ontario, the name and address of the corporation's manager or chief executive in Ontario, the location of the corporation's head office in Ontario, and the name and address of the corporation's agent for service.

The Initial Notice must be signed by a director or officer or a person having knowledge of the affairs of the corporation. The document must be typewritten or printed in block letters.

b. CORPORATIONS INCORPORATED OUTSIDE OF CANADA

If your corporation has been incorporated or continued outside of Canada, you must apply for an extra-provincial licence to carry on business or hold land in Ontario, or to maintain an action in an Ontario court dealing with a contract made by the corporation.

Under the Extra-Provincial Corporations Act, 1984, an extra-provincial corporation carries on business in Ontario if —

(a) it has a resident agent, representative, warehouse office or place where it carries on its business in Ontario;

(b) it holds an interest, otherwise than by way of securities, in real property situated in Ontario; or

(c) it otherwise carries on business in Ontario.

Furthermore, an extra-provincial corporation does not carry on its business in Ontario if it only takes orders or buys or sells goods, wares and merchandise; or if it offers or sells services of any type by use of travellers or through advertising or correspondence.

If you are in any doubt whether or not your corporation carries on business in Ontario, I suggest that you contact a lawyer, or the Companies Branch for help.

The first step toward registration of a corporation incorporated outside of Canada is to clear the corporate name through the Companies Branch. To do this you must obtain from a private search house an Ontario biased or weighted NUANS computer printed search report on the name which is to be cleared by the Companies Branch. The report must be dated not more than 90 days before submission of the application of an extra-provincial licence.

Once the name is cleared, the following documents must be completed and filed with the Companies Branch:

(a) Application for Extra-Provincial Licence in duplicate (see Sample #37)

(b) An appointment of agent for service (see Sample #38)

(c) A Certificate of Status issued under the seal of office and signed by the proper officer (e.g., Director, Corporations Branch) of the jurisdiction to which the corporation is subject and stating the name of the corporation, the date of incorporation, amalgamation or merger, the jurisdiction to which the corporation is subject, and that the corporation is a valid and subsisting corporation

(d) The original cleared NUANS name search report

Both copies of the application for extra-provincial licence must be signed by an officer or director of the corporation, and the name of the corporation must be set out above the signatures. The corporate seal must be affixed to both copies of the application. If the jurisdiction to which the corporation is subject does not require its corporations to have a corporate seal, please indicate so when submitting the application.

When appointing an agent for service of documents, the agent must be a natural person 18 years of age or older residing in Ontario, or a corporation (other than the applicant) having its registered office in Ontario. Where the agent is a corporation, the consent to act as agent for service shall be executed in the name of the corporation under the signature of an officer or director of the corporation which is to act as the agent.

The fee for registering an extra-provincial corporation is $250. The application fee for an existing extra-provincial corporation to obtain an amended extra-provincial licence is $100.

All newly licensed corporations must file an Initial Notice — Form 2 as shown in Sample #36. Or, if the corporation has already obtained a mortmain licence, the corporation must file an Initial Notice — Form 1 as shown in Sample #22.

SAMPLE #36
INITIAL NOTICE OF EXTRA-PROVINCIAL COMPANY
FORM 2

Ministry of Consumer and Commercial Relations	Ministère de la Consommation et du Commerce	Companies Branch	Direction des Compagnies

Ontario

Form 2 - Corporations Information Act
Formule 2 - Loi sur les renseignements exigés des compagnies et associations

NOTE/REMARQUE:
1 Check appropriate box at right/*Cocher la case pertinente à droite.*
2 All items below must be answered/*Prière de remplir toutes les rubriques ci-dessous.*
3 Return form to/*Renvoyer à la:* Examination and Notice Section, Companies Branch
Section des examens et des avis, Direction des compagnies
Ministry of Consumer and Commercial Relations
Ministère de la Consommation et du Commerce
555 Yonge Street. Toronto. Ontario. M7A 2H6

☐ **Initial Notice/** *Avis intial*
OR/OU
☐ **Notice of Change/** *Avis de modification*

---

1. Current corporation Name/*Dénomination sociale actuelle de la compagnie ou de l'association*

I.B. OUTSIDER FABRICATIONS LIMITED

2. Ontario Corporation Number/*Numéro matricule de la compagnie ou de l'association en Ontario*

09876

---

3. Name or style other than the corporate name registered in Ontario (if not applicable state so)/
Dénomination sociale autre que celle enregistrée en Ontario (si cela ne s'impose pas, l'indiquer)

---

4. Former Corporation Name, if changed (if not applicable state so)
Dénomination sociale préalable de la compagnie ou de l'association si celle-ci est différente (si cela ne s'impose pas, l'indiquer)

5. Date Corporation Name Changed
Date de modification de la dénomination sociale

(day/*jour*, month/*mois*, year/*année*)

---

6. Date of incorporation/amalgamation/continuation *Date de constitution/fusion/prorogation*	7. Date commenced business in Ontario *Date du début des activités en Ontario*	8. Date ceased carrying on business in Ontario *Date de cessation des activités en Ontario*
15 01 8– (day/*jour*, month/*mois*, year/*année*)	15 06 8– (day/*jour*, month/*mois*, year/*année*)	(day/*jour*, month/*mois*, year/*année*)

---

9. Current jurisdiction of incorporation/amalgamation/continuation (check ✓ appropriate box)
Ressort actuel de constitution/fusion/prorogation (cocher ✓ la case pertinente)

☒ Alberta ☐ Canada ☐ New Brunswick *Nouveau-Brunswick* ☐ Nova Scotia *Nouvelle-Écosse* ☐ Quebec *Québec* ☐ Yukon

☐ British Columbia *Colombie-Britannique* ☐ Manitoba ☐ Newfoundland *Terre-Neuve* ☐ Prince Edward Island *Île-du-Prince-Édouard* ☐ Saskatchewan ☐ North West Territories *Territoires du Nord-Ouest*

☐ Other *Autre* _____ (Set out name of jurisdiction in full/*Inscrire le nom du ressort au complet*)

---

10. Former jurisdiction of incorporation/amalgamation/continuation (if not applicable state so)
Ressort préalable de constitution/fusion/prorogation (si cela ne s'impose pas, l'indiquer)

---

11. Head Office/registered office address/*Adresse du siège social*

Suite 401
111 North Spadina Road
Edmonton, Alberta

Postal Code *Code postal*
Z 1 P 0 G 0

---

12. Name. (first name. initials and last name) and office address, of chief officer/manager in Ontario
Nom (prénom. initiales et nom) et adresse du bureau du directeur général/gérant en Ontario

Ura A. Korn, 321 Clerks Row, Toronto, Ontario

Postal Code *Code postal*
Z 1 P 0 G 0

---

13. Address of principal office in Ontario/*Adresse du bureau principal en Ontario*

Suite 104
222 South Spadina Road
Toronto, Ontario

Postal Code *Code postal*
Z 1 P 0 G 0

---

14. Name and Office Address of Agent for Service in Ontario/*Nom et adresse du bureau du mandataire aux fins de signification en Ontario*

Andrew Agen, Suite 401, South Spadina Road, Toronto, Ontario

Postal Code *Code postal*
Z 1 P 0 G 0

I/*Je soussigné,* **Ura A. Korn**
Print name in full/*Écrire le nom et prénoms en caractères d'imprimerie*
certify that the information herein contained is true and correct/*atteste que les renseignements précités sont véridiques et exacts.*

Signature ► *Ura A. Korn.*

▼ Check appropriate box/*Cocher la case pertinente*
☒ Director/*Administrateur*
☒ Officer/*Dirigeant*
☐ Other person having knowledge of the affairs of the Corporation/*Autre personne au courant des affaires de la compagnie ou de l'association*

07201 (02/85)

☐ **See Deficiency Notice on reverse side**
Voir l'Avis de renseignements complémentaires ►

118

SAMPLE #37
APPLICATION FOR
EXTRA-PROVINCIAL LICENCE

Ontario Corporation Number

TRANS CODE	Line No.		Stat	Comp Type	Method Incorp.
A	0		O	K	3
18	20		28	29	30

Share	Notice Req'd	Jurisdiction
S	N	
31	32	33 47

Form 1
Extra-
Provincial
Corporations
Act

APPLICATION FOR EXTRA-PROVINCIAL LICENCE

1.

1. The name of the corporation is:

I B OUTSIDER FABRICATIONS LTD.

2. Business name or style, other than the corporate name, under which the corporation is to be licenced in Ontario, if any (if none, state so):

N O N E

3. Jurisdiction to which subject:

New York
(Name of State or Country)

4. Date of incorporation/amalgamation:

25   04   75
(day) (month) (year)

5. Full address of the head or registered office:

Suite 123-321 Big City Street
(Street & Number or R.R. Number & if Multi-Office Building give Room No.)

New York
(Name of Municipality or Post Office)   0 1 2 3 4
Postal Code

New York
(Name of State or Country)

6. The corporation has been authorized to make this application by a resolution passed by the directors of the corporation at a meeting held on:

10   01   8-
(day) (month) (year)

7. Full address (including postal code) of the principal office or chief place of business in Ontario, if determined (if none, state so):

Suite 401-104 Smaller City Street
(Street & Number or R.R. Number & if Multi-Office Building give Room No.)

Toronto
(Name of Municipality or Post Office)   M 1 M 1 M 1
Postal Code

07065

SAMPLE #37 — Continued

2.

8. Chief officer or manager in Ontario, if determined (if none, state so):

Name in full. including all given names	Residence address. giving Street & No. or R.R. No. & Municipality or Post Office and Postal Code
Andrew William Agent	1500 Office Road Toronto, Ontario M2M 2M2

9. The business which the corporation intends to carry on in Ontario is:

The manufacturing, production, buying, selling, exporting, importing, and dealing in wood products and other natural products and metal products and plastics, materials and combinations of any of the aforementioned with any other materials, and the construction, acquisition, maintenance, operation use and management of factories, works and machinery appliances and facilities of any kind whatsoever for any of such or like objects.

10. The corporate existence of the corporation is not limited in any way by statute or otherwise and the corporation is a valid and subsisting corporation.

11. The corporation has capacity to carry on business in Ontario.

12. The corporation has capacity to hold land without any conditions or limitations.

13. The corporation hereby acknowledges that upon the licence being issued the corporation shall be subject to the provisions of the Extra-Provincial Corporations Act, the Corporations Information Act, the Corporations Tax Act and to such further and other legislative provisions as the Legislature of Ontario may deem expedient in order to secure the due management of the corporation's affairs and the protection of its creditors within Ontario.

This application is executed in duplicate.

I B OUTSIDER FABRICATIONS LTD.
(Name of Corporation)

By: _Irving B. Successful_ PRESIDENT
(Signature and Description of Office)

(Corporate Seal)

07065

120

APPOINTMENT OF AGENT

Form 2
Extra-
Provincial
Corporations
Act

Check ✔ the appropriate box

✔ **APPOINTMENT OF AGENT FOR SERVICE** OR

☐ **REVISED APPOINTMENT OF AGENT FOR SERVICE**

Ontario Corporation Number   1.

___I B Outsider Fabrications Ltd.___
(Name of appointing corporation)

_____ (hereinafter called the "Corporation") hereby nominates, constitutes

and appoints ___Robert William Smith___
(Name of agent giving first name, initials and surname)

___123 Attorney Road___   ___Toronto___   ___Ontario___   M 3 M 3 M 3
(Business address of the agent, including Street Number, Suite or Room Number and Municipality)   (Postal Code)

its true and lawful agent for service, to act as such, and as such to sue and be sued, plead and be impleaded in any court in Ontario, and generally on behalf of the corporation within Ontario to accept service of process and to receive all lawful notices and, for the purposes of the corporation to do all acts and to execute all deeds and other instruments relating to the matters within the scope of this appointment. Until due lawful notice of the appointment of another and subsequent agent has been given to and accepted by the Director under the Extra-Provincial Corporations Act, service of process or of papers and notices upon the said agent for service shall be accepted by the corporation as sufficient service.

Dated ___18___ ___04___ ___8-___
(day. month, year)

___I B Outsider Fabrications Ltd.___
(Name of Corporation)

BY: _Irving B. Successful_ ___President___
(Signature)   (Description of Office)

(corporate seal)

Lotta Cash ___Treasurer___
(Signature)   (Description of Office)

CONSENT TO ACT AS AGENT FOR SERVICE

I, ___Robert William Smith___ of ___123 Attorney Road___
(Name of Agent in full)   (Business address including Street

___Toronto___
Number. Suite or Room Number and Municipality)   , Ontario, hereby consent to act as the

Agent for Service in the Province of Ontario of ___I B Outsider Fabrications Ltd.___
(Name of Corporation)

_____

pursuant to the appointment in that behalf executed by the said corporation on the

___18th___ day of ___April___ 19 8- ,

authorizing me to accept service of process and notices on its behalf.

Dated ___18___ ___04___ ___8-___
(day. month, year)

I. M. Witness   _Robert William Smith_
(Signature of witness)   (Signature of the consenting person or corporation)

07064

07065

APPENDIX

DETAILED CHECKLIST OF STEPS TO BE FOLLOWED

1. Select three names for your company.
2. Call or write a private name search company to search your name.
3. Purchase package of forms.
4. Prepare articles and consents.
5. Forward documents to: Companies Branch, 393 University Avenue, Toronto, Ontario.
   (a) Duplicate originals of articles
   (b) Consent forms, if applicable
   (c) Name search report
   (d) Cheque, certified, payable to the Treasurer of Ontario for $250.
6. Receive incorporation documents from Companies Division.
7. Order minute book and seal.
8. Order initial notice from the Companies Branch.
9. Complete banking resolutions and open company bank account.
10. Directors and shareholders resolutions received from typing service, or prepare them.
11. Directors' and shareholders' resolutions signed and filed in minute book along with issued signed share certificates and signed by-laws.
12. Complete registers in minute book.
13. Miscellaneous steps
    (a) Draw up promissory notes for assets transferred to or loans made to the company in initial meetings.
    (b) Contact Retail Sales Department for exemption forms.
    (c) If motor vehicles are involved, visit the Motor Vehicle Branch for transfer forms.
14. File your initial notice.

OTHER TITLES IN THE
SELF-COUNSEL BUSINESS SERIES

STANDARD LEGAL FORMS AND AGREEMENTS FOR CANADIAN BUSINESS
This book has a wide selection of indispensable legal forms and common business agreements ready to be copied onto company letterhead and filled in with the particulars of the arrangement. $14.95

PREPARING A SUCCESSFUL BUSINESS PLAN
A practical guide for small business
This book will guide you through the creation of an exciting and authoritative business plan that will also lay the foundation for a dynamic process of planning and reviewing your business agenda over the long term. $14.95

EMPLOYEE/EMPLOYER RIGHTS
A guide for the Ontario work force
This guide covers many areas of the labor field, including labor standards regarding age of employment, wages, hours of work, rest periods, maternity leave, holidays, and vacations. Unemployment insurance and workers' compensation are also dealt with in detail. $6.95

ASSERTIVENESS FOR MANAGERS
Learning effective skills for managing people
This book explains the uses of assertive skills and provides a step-by-step approach for learning the techniques that are most useful in the business world. Worksheets are included. $9.95

EVERY RETAILER'S GUIDE TO LOSS PREVENTION
Keep your profits! Stop theft!
This book covers planning and implementing a loss prevention program, training employees to spot and foil shoplifters, dealing with internal theft, identifying counterfeit currency, how to act during a robbery, and much more. The authors' proven techniques will help you make your retail business more secure and let you stop paying thieves out of your profits. $12.95

MARKETING YOUR PRODUCT
A planning guide for small business
This practical book explains what a comprehensive marketing plan can do to ensure that your product succeeds in a competitive marketplace. The in-depth checklists included in this book will take you, step-by-step, toward a successful, profitable marketing strategy. $12.95

DOING BUSINESS IN THE U.S.A. UNDER FREE TRADE
How to get the right visa
It is now easier than ever before for Canadians to begin doing business or to expand their markets in the U.S. But in order to do so, you must understand those sections of the agreement and the new procedures that govern such "cross border" dealings. This book is a must for all Canadian businesses that are looking south with an eye to the future. $10.95

MARKETING YOUR SERVICE
A planning guide for small business
There are 32 worksheets for you to develop your own specific marketing plan based on the procedures the authors describe. $12.95

SELLING STRATEGIES FOR SERVICE BUSINESSES
How to sell what you can't see, taste, or touch
The key to success in the service business is selling—and selling yourself. This book provides a step-by-step system for selling your service in a way that you can feel comfortable with. Worksheets are provided for planning and maintenance. $12.95

A PRACTICAL GUIDE TO FINANCIAL MANAGEMENT
Tips and techniques for the non-financial manager
This book goes beyond basic financial control advice to a thorough discussion on how to define information needs to communicate more clearly with your accounting department and make decisions more effectively based on financial information. $7.95

READY-TO-USE BUSINESS FORMS
A complete package for the small business
Running a small business and keeping it in order can be made much simpler if efficient systems are in place and the paperwork is up to date. This handy guide of tear-out forms is just what your small business needs to help you take the worry out of daily record-keeping and routine tasks and put more time into keeping on top of your competitors. $10.95

ORDER FORM
All prices are subject to change without notice. Books are available in book, department and stationery stores, or use this order form. (Please print)

Name _____

Address _____

_____

Charge to:
   ❑Visa   ❑MasterCard

Account Number _____

Validation Date _____

Expiry Date _____

Signature _____

❑**Check here for a free catalogue which outlines all of our publications.**

YES, please send me:

_____copies of **Standard Legal Forms and Agreements for Canadian Business** $14.95

_____copies of **Preparing a Successful Business Plan, $14.95**

_____copies of **Employee/Employer Rights, $6.95**

_____copies of **Assertiveness for Managers, $9.95**

_____copies of **Every Retailer's Guide to Loss Prevention, $12.95**

_____copies of **Marketing Your Product, $12.95**

_____copies of **Doing Business in the U.S.A. Under Free Trade, $10.95**

_____copies of **Marketing Your Service, $12.95**

_____copies of **Selling Strategies for Service Businesses, $12.95**

_____copies of **A Practical Guide to Financial Management, $7.95**

_____copies of **Ready-To-Use Business Forms, $10.95**

Please add $2.50 for postage & handling.
Please send your order to:
Self-Counsel Press
2399 Cawthra Road, Unit 25
Mississauga, Ontario
L5A 2W9